Shareholder Value

Tony Grundy

FINANCE

05.06

- Fast track route to mastering shareholder value

- Covers the key areas of shareholder value, from its role in the management process to its theory, measures and impact on strategy

- Examples and lessons from some of the world's most valuable companies and brands including BP Amoco, Diageo and Manchester United, and ideas from the smartest thinkers including G. Bennett Stewart, Tom Copeland, James M. McTaggart, Roger A. Morin and Sherry L. Jarrell

- Includes a glossary of key concepts and a comprehensive resources guide

The right of Tony Grundy to be identified as the author of this work has been
asserted in accordance with the Copyright, Designs and Patents Act 1988

First published 2002 by
Capstone Publishing (a Wiley company)
8 Newtec Place
Magdalen Road
Oxford OX4 1RE
United Kingdom
http://www.capstoneideas.com

CIP catalogue records for this book are available from the British Library and the
US Library of Congress

ISBN 1-84112-239-4

This book is printed on acid-free paper

Substantial discounts on bulk quantities of Capstone books are available
to corporations, professional associations and other organizations. Please
contact Capstone for more details on +44 (0)1865 798 623 or (fax) +44
(0)1865 240 941 or (e-mail) info@wiley-capstone.co.uk

Contents

Contents

Introduction to ExpressExec

ExpressExec is 3 million words of the latest management thinking compiled into 10 modules. Each module contains 10 individual titles forming a comprehensive resource of current business practice written by leading practitioners in their field. From brand management to balanced scorecard, ExpressExec enables you to grasp the key concepts behind each subject and implement the theory immediately. Each of the 100 titles is available in print and electronic formats.

Through the ExpressExec.com Website you will discover that you can access the complete resource in a number of ways:

» printed books or e-books;
» e-content – PDF or XML (for licensed syndication) adding value to an intranet or Internet site;
» a corporate e-learning/knowledge management solution providing a cost-effective platform for developing skills and sharing knowledge within an organization;
» bespoke delivery – tailored solutions to solve your need.

Why not visit www.expressexec.com and register for free key management briefings, a monthly newsletter and interactive skills checklists. Share your ideas about ExpressExec and your thoughts about business today.

Please contact elound@wiley-capstone.co.uk for more information.

Introduction to Shareholder Value

» Shareholder value focuses on managing corporate and business cash flows in order to optimize the risk and return of shareholders.
» Shareholder value requires managing the system of value-creating activities within a business in alignment with an overall vision.

Shareholder value has become an absolutely central theme in management – both in the 1990s and into the new millennium. Companies like Barclays Bank, BP Amoco, Coca-Cola, Diageo, ICI, and Prudential have made the creation of shareholder value a central, corporate goal.

But like many other modern management terms, shareholder value is to managers, and often at a very senior level, something of a mystery.

We would like to open up your thinking to the power and the potential of shareholder value in this text. Before we begin, let us explore with you a short example from a real life discussion that occurred some years ago.

The author was speaking at an accountants' conference on the topic of shareholder value. An accountant accosted him at the break, muttering, "Zebras, zebras, what can I do with the zebras?" The author wondered for a moment whether he was in a sound state of mind or not. But it appeared – rapidly – that he was. He explained: "I have a client who has a medium-sized stately home. It is open to the public but we are looking to expand our business – to get more punters in. We had the idea of buying two zebras for the park, but I cannot get my head around how to do a business case for the investment decision. What are your thoughts?"

To which the reply was: "Well, what is your vision for the stately home? Are you principally wanting to decorate the gardens a little more? Or are you trying to reposition it as a kind of a mini Chessington Park – which was formerly a zoo but is now a credible theme park with premium rates?

"At Chessington a scaled-down zoo exists but the animals look quiet and bemused at the theme park ride around them – and seem to wince at the screams of the riders, who look down on the animals as they fly through the skies.

"If you really want to do something for the shareholder value of this property then you probably need a mini railway and some monkeys, maybe lions and the odd crocodile or two to spice up the experience. If you can achieve that then your reward could be a) far more customers, b) higher prices, and c) more sales of merchandise, meals, and other objects of dubious value."

The accountant went away looking distinctly happier after this advice. A couple of years later the author actually encountered a park which had a stunning resemblance to this vision.

The lessons from this quick example are that managing shareholder value effectively depends very much on:

» determining the market and competitive position which you really want to achieve;
» investing sufficient resources to bring this off;
» assembling a system of things which work well together in order to leverage customer value – and to capture it; and
» vision and imagination – and not merely number crunching.

At first sight shareholder value and strategy may not seem easy bedfellows. In reconciling these two perspectives, one is reminded of a children's favorite story-book which has two monsters as the main characters – one blue and one red. As the sun goes down one monster says: "Day is ending," whilst the other monster says: "Night is beginning." The two monsters begin a furious argument, hurling stones at each other until they collapse exhausted. Eventually, they realize that they are both in agreement (having used up an entire mountain in their pointless battle).

Shareholder value and strategy are in precisely the same situation – rather than being schizophrenic they are essentially complementary. More than this, each one needs the other to ensure that strategies create, rather than destroy, economic value.

Shareholder value can now be defined as: "The present value of the future cash flows of a company, or of a particular project or decision. This present value can be seen from either a management perspective or from the external shareholders' perspective."

Shareholder value seeks to focus management on pursuing strategies which will help to optimize the future discounted cash flows of all businesses and thus of the corporation.

Managing strategy for shareholder value thus makes finance the essential handmaiden of strategy, rather than being peripheral. Shareholder value can help guide strategy towards choices which produce a virtuous cycle of improving business performance, further opportunities, and higher quality capabilities and resource base.

Definition of Terms:
What Does
"Shareholder Value"
Really Mean?

» "Economic Value Added" ("EVA") and a cash flow perspective give quite different insights and results from accounting profit.
» To assess value creation requires analysis of value and cost drivers, performance drivers, critical success factors, and life cycle effects.

INTRODUCTION

In this chapter we take a look at a number of key terms which have a direct or indirect bearing on shareholder value. These include:

» shareholder value;
» Economic Value Added (EVA);
» Net Present Value (NPV);
» value and cost drivers;
» critical success factors;
» life cycles, finance, competitive advantage – and value;
» performance driver analysis (and "fishbone" analysis); and
» break-even, contribution and economic value.

This section is not heavily quantitative as the key concepts of shareholder value are actually based in economics and strategy – numbers and equations merely capture the end products of our thinking.

SHAREHOLDER VALUE

In Chapter 1, shareholder value was defined as: "The present value of the future cash flows of a company, or of a particular project or decision."

In essence, this definition focuses on shareholder value primarily from a management perspective, as management (at least in theory) *ought* to have a clearer view of these economic prospects than someone on the outside of the company.

Naturally, outsiders too have some view of the company's prospects, and it is their expectations of future performance – combined with signals given by management and from market trends – which determine movements in share price.

Because of the volatility of share prices, proponents of shareholder value management tend to emphasize the importance of getting the internal view of value creation right rather than massaging the external share price. In their view, positive share price movements will follow excellence by the company in generating superior future cash flows, rather than primarily by investor PR exercises or by smoothing the annual profits, earnings per share and dividend growth.

ECONOMIC VALUE ADDED (EVA)

Economic Value Added (EVA) can be defined more specifically as shown in the following equation:

EVA = (rate of return – cost of capital) × capital employed

For example, if a company's net operating profit after tax is £250,000 and its capital is £1,000,000 (and thus its rate of return is 25%), and its cost of capital is 15%, then:

» EVA = (25% − 15%) × £1,000,000
» = 10% × £1,000,000
» = £100,000

EVA is thus residual income (after deducting the cost of capital).

In order to improve EVA, then, one could either generate more operating income, reduce the tax charge, or reduce the cost of capital. The key point of EVA is that it actually provides a better focus for measuring and managing both corporate and business performance than conventional accounting measures.

NET PRESENT VALUE

Net Present Value takes the future stream of cash flows of a business as if it were a project and adjusts for the fact that these cash flows will occur in the future, and will thus have less value than present ones. This lower value can be due to a number of factors, including:

» inflation; plus
» business risk and uncertainty; plus
» the "time value of money."

To explain the latter concept, let me time-travel back to the time my son, James, was eight.

My son James has always been shrewd with his money. By the age of 15 he had lifetime savings of, allegedly, £1500. Once when he was eight I tried to borrow from him.

"James," I said, "could I borrow £20 from you? I will pay you back on Monday when I have gone to a cash machine."

"What will you give me back in return?" he asked.

"What do you want?" I said.

"£30."

If we take the above example, James' time value of money demanded a 50% return over a two-day period. His "cost of capital" appeared (at that point) to be many tens of thousands of per cent.

Whilst not all investors are as aggressive as my son was (otherwise capital markets would seize up), the case nicely illustrates that over and above pure riskiness, investors still need a return. Combined with inflation, the time value of money (sometimes called "investor's marginal rate of time preference") is the same as "the risk-free rate" of return.

But where does value come from? Let us now look at value added and costs drivers.

VALUE AND COST DRIVERS

Turning next to value drivers, our definition of a value driver is as follows: "Anything either internal or external to a business which directly or indirectly contributes to cash inflows."

Within value drivers we include environmental factors such as the strength of customer demand for a product – and its perceived value within the customer's value system.

A cost driver is: "Anything either internal or external to a business which directly or indirectly contributes to cash outflows."

Some more obvious value drivers are:

» sales growth – this drives cash inflows and helps produce economies of scale; and

» competitive rivalry – which is an indirect value driver. For example, acute competitive rivalry can often lead to discounting, price wars, and severe reduction in margins.

Margin is a most important value driver which follows on from competitive rivalry. Margin levels are particularly sensitive to the degree of competitive rivalry in the market.

Some value drivers are negative and we call them "value destroyers." A recent example of shareholder value destruction is that of BT.

According to the *Sunday Times* (May 13, 2001), BT wrote off £3bn on the value of a German acquisition and sought a £5.9bn rights issue to reduce its debt mountain to a more modest £20bn. During the first quarter of 2001 BT lost over £1bn due to these problems and its adventure into third generation mobile telecommunications.

CRITICAL SUCCESS FACTORS

Value and cost drivers are managed by meeting critical success factors.

Critical success factors can be defined as: "The areas in which an organization must excel to outperform competition and thus deliver shareholder value."

Let us now look briefly at the case of the Millennium Dome.

The Dome – critical success factors and value drivers

In the very late 1990s, the UK government decided to celebrate the Millennium with an exciting, visionary project. Situated in Docklands, the Dome was set up to be a magnificent experience – a huge structure housing themed exhibits. The critical success factors for this project were:

» it would be finished well in time (in fact, there were major delays);
» its opening would run smoothly (which it did not);
» it would be well managed (the organization which ran the Dome – The Millennium Experience Company – was afflicted by a number of top management departures, and considerable acrimony);
» it would be such an unbelievable (and relevant) experience that the word of mouth effect would draw in a substantial proportion of the UK population – 12 million people – in just one year. (In reality, only a fraction of the UK population that was originally assumed actually came. Many of those who came were attracted by discounted tickets.)

Two critical success factors which were required to manage the Dome's value and cost drivers well were:

» the quality of service at the Dome – for example, smooth crowd flows and reasonable queues (again, there were substantial queues around certain bottlenecks – like The Body Zone); and

» the project would be finished on time, so that there would be no cost overruns (again, the cost of the Dome – around £758mn – exceeded the original budget).

LIFE CYCLES, FINANCE, COMPETITIVE ADVANTAGE – AND VALUE

Both life cycle effects and competitive advantage can also be related to financial performance as follows.

Conventional life cycle analysis suggests a number of stages which run more or less sequentially over time: emerging, growth, maturing, decline, renewal. Each stage demands a different competitive strategy and a different focus of investment.

Market-related life cycle effects also have implications for a company's financial strategy, helping you to derive financing needs and net funding requirements.

A company's net funding requirements comprise forecast net cash inflows from existing operations (less any planned disposals) and deliberate and emergent investment decisions. These funding requirements, and a company's financing mix, will develop over the life cycles (see Table 2.1).

Table 2.1 Shareholder value and life cycle effects.

Stages of life cycle	Investment requirement	Cost of capital	Gearing*	Retained earnings as a finance source	Dividend policy
Emerging	Very high	Very high	Low–high	Low	No dividends
Growth	Very high	Low–medium	Low–medium	Medium	Low dividends
Maturity	Low–medium	Medium	Medium	High	High dividends
Decline	Possibly negative	Medium–high	Medium–high	High	Special dividends (capital buy-back)
Renewal	Low–Medium	Medium	Medium–high	High	Medium dividends

*Gearing is defined as the ratio of debt to equity

In the emerging phase, gearing might be low where a company is simply unable to obtain significant borrowings – as loans. Or, it may be high because it has secured venture capital. However, much of this funding may be in effect quasi-capital (for instance, where loans can be converted to shares) requiring a high return because of the high business risk. Hence the cost of capital will be invariably high.

Second, in the growth phase, the cost of capital may be substantially lower, as the business has become established and because investors perceive it to be an attractive venture to invest in. Once again, there is a high importance of revenue planning, and of both product and customer profitability during this phase.

Third, in the maturity and decline phases, investment requirements decline, dividends rise as a proportion of earnings, and there may even be special dividends declared (in effect capital repaid). This reduces the capital base and thus helps improve return on capital. There is increasing pressure to achieve a better rate of return in these phases through better product and customer profitability and cost management.

We can now relate competitive advantages and their financial impact directly (see Table 2.2).

PERFORMANCE DRIVERS

In this sub-section we look at both performance driver analysis and fish-bone analysis which help us to visualize value creation and destruction more effectively.

First, a useful way of analyzing business and financial performance is to identify the key performance drivers using a tailored version of "force field" analysis. In a force field analysis each force (positive or negative) is drawn in proportion to its perceived importance and its direction of positive or negative impact.

A performance driver (an upward arrow) is any factor (externally or internally) which will positively impact on financial performance. Performance drivers here are drawn as upward arrows and performance brakes are shown as downward arrows. Figure 2.1 illustrates this with reference to some of the perceived external and internal performance drivers of Rover cars, based on external data around late 1995.

Table 2.2 The impact of competitive advantage on the value drivers.

Competitive advantage	Sales volumes	Prices	Value drivers Discounting	Margin generation	Cost base
Brand	Increased volume	Higher prices	Avoids discounting	Facilitates new products	Neutral impact
Market share	Increased volume	May require lower prices	May require discounting	May improve (or not)	Improves economies of scale
Product value for money	Increased volume	Increases prices	Avoids discounting	Positive impact	May push costs up
Innovation	Higher increases in volume (existing and new businesses)	May enhance prices	Avoids discounting	Improved margins	Unnecessary costs avoided
Customer service	Increased volume	Probably neutral	Avoids discounting	Neutral impact	Some extra costs but less advertising?

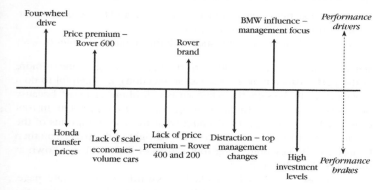

Fig. 2.1 Rover cars – performance (around 1995).

Doing a performance driver analysis to understand the underlying drivers of financial performance can (and should) be married to qualitative analysis. In Rover's case, it would have been interesting to analyze, for example, just how much value was being created by its four wheel drive range, or how much value was being diluted or destroyed (annually, in millions of pounds) through Honda's transfer prices of platforms to Rover.

By 1999 Rover Group's performance drivers had turned strongly negative when it made a massive loss of over £900mn. These performance brakes included:

» over-positioning of the new Rover 75;
» costs of replacing Honda technology;
» cultural differences between Rover and BMW;
» much increased investment (to improve its range); and
» the very strong UK exchange rate.

Performance driver analysis can be used to:

» understand what underpins an existing business unit's performance;
» understand the past performance of an acquisition target more effectively;

» target *future* performance of a business area, and to focus its investment on shareholder value creation; and

» match its inherent characteristics with financing requirements.

Where a business area is under-performing (according to one or more of the performance brakes – see last sub-section), it is helpful to do a root cause analysis (sometimes known as a "fishbone analysis" because of its shape) to expose the underlying causes of the problem. In root cause analysis you begin by defining what the core symptoms of the problem are. This is then written to the far right of the page. You then brainstorm the key underlying root causes of the problem, shown as the "bones" of the "fishbone."

Each cause can then be worked backwards on a separate page. Obviously some root causes might be more fundamental than the others, so you might decide to be selective in your analysis. Finally, some root causes will be the "end of the line." An example of this might be, quite simply, "Senior management is not particularly competent" (unless of course you want to query why that is so).

Figure 2.2 now illustrates a root cause (or fishbone) analysis of a particular under-performing business.

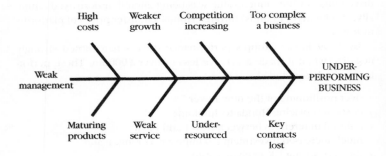

Fig. 2.2   Fishbone analysis.

BREAK-EVEN, CONTRIBUTION AND ECONOMIC VALUE

Break-even analysis helps managers to anticipate the activity threshold level at which a business (or a specific product) begins to make money. Generally, break-even analysis presumes a basic level of "fixed costs." It also presumes that the extra margin between sales revenue and variable cost is a relative constant. This difference between incremental sales revenue and variable cost is known as "contribution." The break-even point is that level of sales volume at which the business makes zero profit, because total revenues equal total costs.

Break-even analysis should be used with "gap" analysis.

"Gap analysis analyses the difference between our current performance and that required to generate shareholder value (or the 'value gap')."

Conventional break-even analysis is somewhat limited in its value. Some of its major implicit assumptions can be challenged as follows.

» *Fixed costs are actually "fixed"*: Not only will they shift over time (and be semi-variable) but also in the longer term you would argue that "no costs are fixed," as you can reinvent your business model.
» *Variable costs vary in a linear fashion*: This is unlikely. They may well increase at a lower rate than turnover (due to economies of scale and experience curve effects).
» *Price remains constant*: This may not be the case. The "fixed price" assumption appears abstract when we consider actual competitive behavior. Frequently sales staff may reduce price to gain market share and volume, or introduce discounts or other less obvious incentives (such as special payment terms) or service concessions (sources of value dilution or destruction). All of these tactics reduce revenues or increase costs, or both, raising the break-even point.

The crucial point here is that "break-even" is just one milestone on the road to delivering economic value. Achieving "break-even" does not mean that you are delivering a decent rate of return on capital. Also, as break-even is typically based on accounting-based measures, it does not represent genuine shareholder value creation.

CONCLUSION

Whilst EVA and NPV are crucial in providing more objective measures for shareholder value, there are also a number of more qualitative terms which are equally important. It is said that there are perhaps around 100 adjustments necessary to adjust accounting results to various measures of EVA or "economic profit." We would do well to avoid getting bogged down in these.

The sections on value and cost drivers, life cycle effects, and competitive advantage illustrate well the need to keep the "numbers" side of these things in perspective.

KEY LEARNING POINTS

» Quantitative assessment of the EVA of a business (or its Net Present Value) are only as good as the underlying thinking and assumptions about the business.
» To tease out and challenge this thinking we need to draw on the concepts of:
  » value and cost drivers;
  » competitive advantage;
  » life cycle effects; and
  » performance driver analysis.
» Break-even (as is conventionally thought of), is not neutral, but actually reflects shareholder value destruction.

The Evolution of Shareholder Value

» Shareholder value management came out of financial theory, economics, and strategic management.
» It is used by major corporations to manage corporate and business performance.
» Increasingly its ideal application gives equal weight to both quantitative and qualitative analysis.

In this chapter we move more into the financial and quantitative aspects of managing shareholder value. The essence of managing for shareholder value is that.

» Capital is not "free" – it is provided by the capital market on the condition that managers can – in the long term – beat its cost.
» Capital is not cheap – because businesses are risky, the cost of capital is higher than the rate of return on deposit accounts or gilts.
» The longer the time between investing and recouping outlays, the greater future cash inflows need to be – so money has a time value.
» Achieving accounting profit does not necessarily mean that a business (or a specific project) will add to shareholder value. Instead we must look at "economic profit," this being concerned with net operating cash flow generation – less the costs of investment to generate and sustain those cash flows.
» Where a business genuinely sets out to manage economic profit rather than its accounting profit, in the longer term (other things being equal – like no sudden impact of terrorist attacks) this ought to lead to greater increases in shareholder value.
» Managing for shareholder value does not mean an inevitable focus on short-termism – in fact it actually enables longer-term decision-making rather than managing primarily through short-term budgets. This occurs by analyzing discounted cash flows.
» Specific business decisions can add, dilute, or potentially even destroy shareholder value – and therefore need to be thought through both strategically and financially in order to generate and sustain economic value (see especially Chapter 10).

Management processes which are important include conventional planning, budgeting, investment appraisal, performance review, and rewards and recognition processes. These need to be fundamentally thought through again so that shareholder value imperatives are reflected in everyday routines. BP Amoco, for example, took many years to bed down these changes (from 1987 to 1995), and the full impact of shareholder value creation was felt only between 1995 and 2001 (see Chapter 7).

Figure 3.1 summarizes the key ingredients of managing for shareholder value.

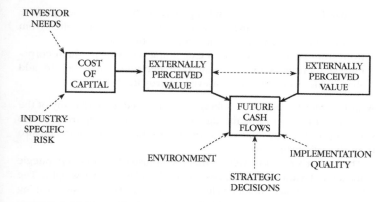

Fig. 3.1   Managing for shareholder value.

» The cost of capital is determined by investor needs, industry-specific risk, and the expected prospects for the company.

» The cost of capital is used to put a value on the businesses and to assess any gap between the sum of these values and the external value of the company.

» Economic profit is the basis for this internal valuation, which is, in turn, dependent on future business performance.

» Future business performance (and thus economic value creation) depends upon the appropriateness of key management decisions such as new investment (see Chapter 4), acquisitions (see Chapter 5), alliances, and divestment, and also upon the external environment and the quality of strategy implementation.

The theory of shareholder value management comes from a number of sources:

» from financial economics, especially from thinking about how capital markets operate – especially when achieving an "efficient" allocation of finance between businesses – to extract good and appropriate returns for shareholders;

» from industrial economics, and in particular the understanding of the possibilities of generating economic rent (or superior profits) from imperfect and often localized market conditions; and

» from strategic management, in examining the way in which corporate and business management take decisions – whether to add shareholder value, dilute it, or even destroy it.

Whilst financial economic thinking has come to dominate many of the texts on shareholder value management, there was an important, if less vocal, input from the industrial economics school of thought, and also from strategic management.

The author's personal view is that the industrial economic/strategic management views and finances should be given equal weight. The introduction of shareholder value management as a decision-making framework should be (if anything) biased towards helping managers to think more conceptually (and frequently qualitatively) about shareholder value creation – rather than succumbing to an over-emphasis on the quantitative – and upon "dealing the numbers."

But perhaps these first three schools of thought are incomplete and we might also need to take on board an important fourth one – "The Implementation Perspective." Past research suggests that perhaps the most critical constraint on shareholder value management lies in overcoming the hurdles to implementation.

As you will see in the BP Amoco case (Chapter 7), the organizational mind-set (or "paradigm"), together with the incumbent control systems, is the largest and most daunting hurdle to getting the real value out of shareholder value management. But for the early origins of shareholder value management we perhaps have to go back to the "stewardship" principle of financial accounting.

Due to a number of financial calamities (for example the "South Sea Bubble" nearly 300 years ago), it was recognized that enterprises needed to account for their assets and liabilities, their profits and losses at each calendar year end. Although primitive in its accuracy and richness, accounting profit became the established and legitimate measure through which business and corporate performance was judged.

When the author qualified as an accountant – over 25 years ago – this simple concept had become quite an industry. Any new accountant had to memorize the voluminous details of many "Standard Statements of Accounting Practice" (or "SSAPs"). But whilst accountants (in practice) sought to become more and more efficient in getting the numbers precisely wrong, by the mid/late 1980s a number of thinkers began to question – and quite aggressively – whether compiling traditional account reports and accounts was actually the right thing to do at all!

The main thrust was then from financial economics, which argued that cash flow generation was the only sensible measure against which shareholder value creation could be judged. In unison, industrial economists hinted that to a large extent economic value creation was largely down to the competitive interaction (successful or otherwise) between a business and its markets.

Strategic management was then able to translate the ideas of industrial economics into frameworks for understanding the life cycle effects, as we saw in Chapter 2 (and their impact on value creation) of industries and also of a company's own unique competitive position.

So by 1986 the time was ripe for the first real synthesis of Shareholder Value Management.

Alfred Rappaport's major book on shareholder value[1] was the first major synthesis of financial economics, industrial economics, and (to a more limited extent) strategic management. Rappaport was also involved in devising value-based management software – so that financial analysis of stakeholder value could be achieved effectively.

Around the same time, Marakon Associates, a US value-based strategy consultancy was formed, and began to work with major US companies. Its goal was to help them refocus decision-making from accounting-based measures. Once some major blue-chip companies like Coca-Cola began to adopt the new decision-making and performance control framework, value-based management began to catch on elsewhere.

Marakon Associates have been joined in this market by the traditional consulting firms like McKinsey, and more latterly by some of the key large accounting firms – although after a significant time lag. Marakon still operate very much on a niche consultancy – without armies of consultants. Their major UK projects have included parts of ICI, BP Amoco, and Prudential.

Following Rappaport's early book, over the next few years there was a flurry of further publications (which we expand on in Chapter 8).

These included Bernard Reimann's book,[2] which emphasized to a far greater extent the need to think through the impact of industrial economics in value creation and also the impact of strategic management input. Copeland *et al.*'s *Valuation: Measuring and Managing the Value of Companies*[3] (nominally associated with McKinsey) is perhaps at the other end of the spectrum, being theoretical and computational. It is, however, a very comprehensive guide to the "how to"s and the "do"s and "don't"s of economic value-based computation.

A major lift-off in the subject came when the catchy title of "Economic Value Added" ("EVA") was coined by G. Bennett Stewart,[4] a partner in the corporate finance/strategy boutique firm of Stern Stewart. This writer combined an evangelical approach to shareholder value with writing which is surprisingly digestible, especially considering its roots are in applied financial economies.

Reading these last two books will give you a great deal of enlightenment on financial economics, but quite limited insight on industrial economics and probably very little indeed on linkages with strategic management.

A further stream of development came out of strategic management/strategic decision-making enquiry. The research of Barwise *et al.*[5] (in 1988) into strategic investment decisions documented how major industrial decisions were often made in a fragmentary way. There was relatively little focus on the links between the investment decision and its strategic context, and the key value and cost drivers. Regrettably Barwise *et al.* had few suggestions as to how their difficulties could be overcome.

Following Marsh, during 1988–1992 the author researched strategic decision-making involving major investment decisions at four major organizations: Rolls Royce Aeroengines, IDV (now part of Diageo – see also Chapter 7), the Post Office (Counters Business), and London Underground.[6] My key findings were as follows.

» One of the main impediments was that the strategy itself was frequently not clear enough or well articulated enough for it to be understood how it could generate or sustain shareholder value creation.

» When "doing the numbers" managers often failed to realize the need to align many factors (to give both the necessary and sufficient conditions) in order to generate value.

» "Uncertainty" clouded both the strategic appraisal and the appraisal of shareholder value. But a closer examination revealed that much of this uncertainty was down to an inability or unwillingness to imagine the future – for instance using scenario-based techniques of storytelling.

» Many areas of value were labeled as "intangible" (or as non-measurable). But in most cases some approximate "feel" for potential value could be made for these unquantified areas of value.

» Managers appeared unwilling to abandon more traditional ways of measuring corporate performance (through accounting profit) because control and reward systems in their organization were very sticky culturally. It was also difficult politically to change these. Knowing this, managers were therefore inhibited from adopting decision-making and planning processes towards shareholder value management.

The above suggested that for shareholder value management to be implemented effectively a more balanced and holistic process was needed so that strategy and financial analysis could be integrated. This would need to be based on extensive education – vital to making it a success rather than a finance-department based, number crunching initiative.

Following on in this mode of thinking McTaggart et al.[7] produced a balanced account of how value-based management could be implemented by integrating strategic and financial analysis into a single process. This book follows very closely the process of Marakon Associates. Further applications of this approach with focus on some more specific management applications include:

» acquisitions (especially with Haspeslagh and Jemison);[8]
» strategic cost management (see Shank and Govindarajan);[9]
» matching sources of finance and investors' needs to life cycle and competitive effects (Ward);[10] and
» using value-based management to enrich management accounting/ performance analysis (Ward).[11]

Since the early 1990s, whilst a number of further texts have appeared, there have been relatively few new additions to these fundamental approaches, save for attempts to gain a more dynamic view of shareholder value creation over time. This is reflected by work on "value migration"[12] (see also the Manchester United case study in Chapter 7) or the use of scenario-related techniques.[13]

Slywotzky's notion of value migration is in itself a most interesting one. Slywotzky's argument is that due to shifts in industrial structure, in the way in which value can be created and also delivered to customers, value can migrate. This invites changes in the company's business model (where and how value is created – and with what resource) and mind-set.

Typical influences which have created the possibility of value migration include:

» telephone-based delivery;
» brands becoming more "stretchy" (like Virgin, Easygroup and even Tesco);
» other new technologies being applied;
» new market/product configurations which remove redundancy within the resource base or processes, or which actually take away specific sources of "value destruction" (sometimes known humorously as "VD" – value destruction can occur through either customer or competitor complacency, or both); and
» e-commerce delivery.

The final pieces of the jigsaw puzzle come from strategic management debates, especially between the idea of "deliberate" strategy (Ansoff,[14] Porter[15]) versus "emergent" (Mintzberg[16]). We have already made the point that often the strategy itself is an incomplete basis for computing future cash flows and shareholder value. This means that more thinking may be required about the strategy.

A deliberate strategy is one which sets out a very clear strategic direction and an idea of how to execute it – alongside a well-thought-through analysis of the external environment. A deliberate strategy can be either realized or actually unrealized, depending upon how clever and innovative it is, competitor activity, and environmental change. External competitive change can be understood by using Porter's five competitive forces,[17] which include buyer power, rivalry, and substitutes.

Deliberate strategies, which are well tested, well prioritized, and well resourced, often have a higher-than-average chance of creating shareholder value.

Emergent strategies are defined as ones which are merely patterns in a past series of decisions and actions. The problem with emergent strategies is that here shareholder value creation tends to be frustrated. Emergent strategies are frequently reworked, abandoned, and resources then wasted – and staff become demoralized. With relatively few, "lucky" exceptions, emergent strategies tend to dilute or even destroy shareholder value.

In addition to these core forms of strategy, we can also expand this to three further forms, namely:

» "submergent": here the strategy has drifted off course, and is beginning to fail;
» "emergency": here management has gone purely tactical, and is very likely to destroy shareholder value through short-term and ill-conceived action; and
» "detergent": here management focuses on rationalizing the strategy and upon preparing the basis for a future, more robust competitive strategy.

THE STRATEGY MIX AND SHAREHOLDER VALUE

The impact of the various "forms of strategy" on shareholder value – (sometimes known as the "strategy mix") is illustrated in the following summary.

Deliberate strategy

» *Preconditions*: Environmental analysis; Competitive analysis; Value based analysis
» *Value added*: Competitive surprise; Resource concentration
» *Value diluted/destroyed*: Inappropriate decisions; Environmental change

Emergent strategy

» *Preconditions*: External uncertainty; Fluid strategic thinking
» *Value added*: Flexibility of response; Big commitment deferred
» *Value diluted/destroyed*: Resources diluted; Inconsistencies between strategies

Submergent strategy

» *Preconditions*: Past deliberate strategy; Unwise emergent strategy
» *Value added*: Not a lot!
» *Value diluted/destroyed*: Delayed new thinking; Excessive investment

Emergency strategy

» *Preconditions*: Strategic drift/poor decisions; Tactical tendencies
» *Value added*: Not at all!
» *Value diluted/destroyed*: Operational damage; Demoralized staff

Detergent strategy review

» *Preconditions*: Post strategic; New review leadership
» *Value added*: Migration out of value destruction; Clearing the decks – for the future
» *Value diluted/destroyed*: Costs of disruption and change; Commitment to outdated strategy

THE EVOLUTION OF SHAREHOLDER VALUE MANAGEMENT

Having discussed the evolution of shareholder value theory we are now in a position to map over time the evolution of shareholder value management.

» *1970s*: applied financial economies; industrial economics; corporate planning models
» *1980s*: EVA; corporate finance theory; application to acquisitions
» *Early 1990s*: value-based management processes; strategic investment option theory; strategic cost management
» *Late 1990s*: value migration; scenarios.

To illustrate the ideas in this chapter we can draw usefully from a short case on Amazon.com.

AMAZON.COM

Amazon.com was set up in the mid/late 1990s by an entrepreneur called Bezos, as an innovative bookseller using the Internet as, in effect, a virtual retail network. By relying on centralized order fulfillment Amazon.com could provide a much wider catalogue of books than usual at competitive prices.

With hype over Internet development, Amazon.com was able to persuade many investors to back what subsequently turned out to be a very high risk venture. Lured by the prospect of big, quick, and easy capital gains in the form of an ever-increasing share price, investors jumped on the bandwagon.

Unlike its ailing Internet brethren, Amazon.com was able to capture a significant share of the market. Indeed in sales revenue terms, its success was impressive. Unfortunately, however, its underlying business model did not appear – at least in the short and medium term – able to support the hike in its share price.

As Amazon.com promised no early profits and no early dividend stream, its investors were drawn into the following train of thought:

1 this is an inherently uncertain business;
2 and one with a business model which will not necessarily deliver shareholder value.

As Amazon.com was some way from delivering shareholder value (actually a very long way), there was little point in looking for profit, positive cash flow, and shareholder value within the foreseeable future or otherwise.

Amazon.com's initial vision was therefore to become the world's virtual supplier of books, accomplishing this through cost leadership, underpinned by Internet technology.

» The competitive forces for this market, (given the cosy existence of substitute channels and the higher propensity for customers to shop around) severely limit margin potential.
» Amazon.com's aggressive discounting strategy leaves it with little room to widen its margins.

» Whilst Amazon.com is a thrusting, technology-led, and innovative company, will it have the necessary commercial and financial acumen to turn this apparent market success into real shareholder value? (For instance, currently Amazon.com's 1999 accounts contain a very long list of major uncertainties – but there is very little mention of countermeasures to deal with these.)

Amazon.com's total market capitalization has been as high as $5–10bn in the past few years (though not recently). This is hard to square with the above analysis of the company's growth drivers external and internal, which are uncertain, and the longer-term competitive structure of the industry, which is a tough one.

Amazon.com provides a startling example of how growth can actually destroy rather than create shareholder value, underlying the need to seek value-based, sustainable growth.

The impact of growth on the company's value and cost drivers must therefore be thought through, (see Chapter 10). Without this, the potential for economic profit may not be challenged and unsustainable and value-destroying growth may result. Amazon.com highlights the need to pursue a balance of growth objectives rather than too narrow a set (like market share).

This brief analysis also suggests a number of potentially fruitful lines of enquiry (possibly "breakthroughs") for Amazon.com, including:

» a move upmarket into Internet-based sales of higher value and higher margin products and services;
» reducing costs in the core business to improve margins, and repackaging and repositioning its pricing and the service offering to capture more value and increase margins; and
» resetting expectations of future earnings with key external and internal stakeholders to more realistic levels.

To summarize, shareholder value management focuses on:

» cash flow generation (EVA) as a key area for management focus;
» the "time value of money" when evaluating corporate and business strategies – rational investors are said to prefer money now versus in the future;

» shifting from conventional, historical measures of financial return such as "return on capital" (as measured by both the profit and loss account and the balance sheet – which can be misleading measures of financial performance) towards cash flow based measures; because the historical accounting measures are based on non-cash adjustments and are typically derived from historic or one year's figures, they do not help us much when evaluating longer-term strategic options – from a shareholder value perspective.

CONCLUSION

Shareholder value is an absolutely critical concept in the modern management process. It combines an entrepreneurial focus with the strategic vision about markets, competition, competencies, and resource management to take both a long- and short-term view of the business.

KEY LEARNING LESSONS

» Shareholder value hinges just as much on strategic vision as it does on "doing the numbers."
» Shareholder value crystallizes when resources are well aligned with a powerful external competitive position – and when strategies are implemented well.
» Key business decisions need to target not only beating the cost of capital, but also generally a "super-return" even beyond that.
» Whilst understanding and measuring the cost of capital is of importance, even more important is understanding how value is created and captured by the business.
» Managing shareholder value through EVA can give a very different picture of wealth creation of a business than conventional accounting profit measurement.

NOTES

1 Rappaport, A. (1986) *Creating Shareholder Value*. The Free Press, New York.

2 Reimann, B. (1990) *Managing for Value: A Guide to Value-Based Strategic Management*. Basil Blackwell, Oxford.

3 Copeland, T., Koller, T. & Murrin, J. (1990) *Valuation: Measuring and Managing the Value of Companies*. John Wiley & Sons, New York.

4 Stewart, G. Bennett III (1991) *The Quest for Value –The EVA Management Guide*. Harperbusiness, New York.

5 Barwise, P., Marsh, P. & Wensley, R. (1989) "Must Finance and Strategy Clash?" *Harvard Business Review*, Sept–Oct, 85–90.

6 Grundy, A.N. (1992) *Corporate Strategy and Financial Decisions*. Kogan Page, London.

7 McTaggart, J.M., Kontes, P.W. & Mankins, M.C. (1994) *The Value Imperative*. Free Press, Macmillan, New York.

8 Haspeslagh, P.C. & Jemison, D.B. (1991) *Managing Acquisitions*. The Free Press, Macmillan, New York.

9 Shank, J.K. & Govindarajan, V. (1993) *Strategic Cost Management*. The Free Press, Macmillan, New York.

10 Ward, K. (1993) *Corporate Financial Strategy*. Butterworth-Heinemann, Oxford.

11 Ward, K. (1993) *Strategic Management Accounting*. Butterworth-Heinemann, Oxford.

12 Slywotzky, A.J. (1996) *Value Migration*. Harvard Business School Press, Boston.

13 Grundy, A.N. & Brown, L. (2001) *Be Your Own Strategy Consultant*. International Thomson Publishing, London.

14 Ansoff, H.I. (1965) *Corporate Strategy*. McGraw-Hill, New York.

15 Porter, E.M. (1985) *Competitive Advantage*. Free Press, New York.

16 Mintzberg, H. (1994) "The Fall and Rise of Strategic Planning." *Harvard Business Review*, Jan–Feb, 107–114.

17 Porter, *ibid.* and Mintzberg, *ibid.*

Shareholder Value in Practice – The Strategic Investment Decision

» Strategic investment decisions are one of the main vehicles for shareholder value creation.

» The investment process requires close integration of strategic and financial analysis, otherwise the resultant Net Present Value (NPV) can prove illusory.

» Focusing on shareholder value entails careful testing of competitive assumptions together with a thorough exploration and testing of options.

Strategic investment decisions are a major area of shareholder value management. Strategic investment decisions can add major value to the business – or destroy it.

These decisions are impacted on by both external and internal uncertainty. Paradoxically, traditional finance theory has almost been to pretend that such uncertainty does not exist. By focusing almost exclusively on the need to quantify value (and with precision), financial theory has turned investment appraisal virtually into a ritual.

A strategic investment decision is thus "a major cash outlay to increase, enhance, or defend a company's competitive position with a view to generating longer-term cash flow."

In this chapter we examine the thinking which needs to occur not only to appraise a specific investment decision but also to evaluate the value of business unit strategy. First, we take a closer look at the decision process involved in strategic investment decisions.

Any strategic investment decision can be managed through the following process:

» *definition*: define the scope and focus of the strategic investment project, including its strategic objectives and context;
» *options*: explore critical options for the decision;
» *targeting and collecting data*: target the data required, having done a first-cut review of the kind of external and internal assumptions which will need to be made about key value drivers;
» *assumptions*: collect and evaluate data through formulating the external and internal assumptions. Test these assumptions, revisit the key options, and work up contingency plans;
» *business case*: present the business case and, where feasible, refine the program to add more value at less cost and at lowest risk; and
» *controls*: translate the business case into monitoring measures and controls.

DEFINITION OF THE DECISION

If we examine the definition of the decision (or program) more clearly, we soon realize there are many problems in defining the unit of analysis. Is it a particular strategic development project or a more broadly based program? Where there are many and complex interdependencies it is frequently easier and better to evaluate the financials at the level of a set of projects ("the strategic project set").

For example, if we look at the example of investing in a fleet of supermarket trolleys, one should first ask: "What is the most appropriate unit of analysis of the investment project, or program?" Although the costs of a new trolley fleet could be quantified, the benefits might be less tangible, for many of these benefits relate to customer value. The effectiveness of a supermarket trolley is of importance – from a customer perspective. This importance is part of the "total service" effect – in combination with other programs including:

» the level of staff service and friendliness to customers generally; and
» the provision of other physical conveniences to support the shopping experience (including crêche, café, and hygiene facilities).

So it would be inappropriate to consider the investment in supermarket trolleys in relative isolation. This total customer service package is thus the strategic project set.

Figure 4.1 now suggests that you first need to question whether the project is self-contained or not. Only if it is self-contained can you determine that it should be analyzed as a distinct project.

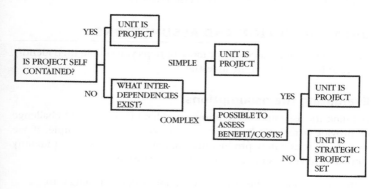

Fig. 4.1 What is the unit of analysis?.

Next, you need to ask whether there are many interdependencies, and if so, whether these are simple (thus enabling them to be analyzed as a discrete project) or complex. If they are complex, then the final question is: "Is it easy to do a cost/benefit analysis of them?" If it is not easy, then you should not analyze this as a separate project. Instead, you should analyze it amongst part of a higher level set of projects, or the "strategic project set."

OPTIONS

There are invariably many different options for defining a strategic investment project and not merely the most obvious one – for instance:

» might the strategic objective be achieved through organic or through acquisitive activity?
» is it more appropriate to move very quickly or slowly?
» is it worthwhile piloting development prior to making a bigger commitment (usually it is)?
» should commitment be delayed until there is a sufficiently strong implementation capability, enough resource, and the right timing?
» can the project's key objectives be fulfilled at lower cost or with more flexibility through an alternative option?
» if we go ahead with this particular project, what other options (present and future) does this decision foreclose?

DATA COLLECTION AND ASSUMPTIONS

Once you have identified one or more options you should then identify the cash flow impact of the investment.

Evaluating the assumptions

Defining the assumptions requires considerable debate and challenge to provide a realistic basis for a business case. For example, if we were looking at a new product investment decision we might identify a number of key assumed/value drivers, for instance:

» the new product adds superior customer value, enabling it to:
  » sustain volumes (in existing customers); and

» increase margins (slightly);
» this enables new customers to be captured; and
» the level of competitive rivalry is a value driver (as this might increase or reduce prices).

Cost drivers also include:

» unit costs, which might be influenced by levels of activity through economies of scale; and
» the cost of new product development.

Frequently, investment cases omit or take for granted many of the implicit external assumptions. Although incremental sales volumes, prices, and margins are invariably spelt out, less thoroughly examined are factors like competitive behavior and key elements of the customer's business value system.

Analyzing importance and uncertainty of assumptions

One way of now testing the external and internal assumptions is by using a qualitative uncertainty–importance grid (see Fig. 4.2, derived from Mitroff and Linstone).[1] Using this grid, managers can plot key assumptions driving the value of the strategic investment decision. These can be external or internal, and hard or soft assumptions.

Once assumptions are carefully and skillfully defined, it is possible to debate the relative importance and uncertainty of these various assumptions.

At the beginning of the investment appraisal, key assumptions are likely to be mapped in the due North and North-East quadrants. Upon testing it is quite common to find one or more assumptions moving over to the danger zone in the South-East.

The uncertainty–importance grid is therefore a vital tool for evaluating assumptions prior to undertaking key financial sensitivities. This tool helps focus these sensitivities towards the critical uncertainties (for example, to new competitor entry). A sensitivity is defined as being the financial impact from a change in either a value or cost driver.

Not all assumptions will be within a company's influence. Figure 4.3 now helps us to replot these and establish which we should focus on (those towards the bottom and far right).

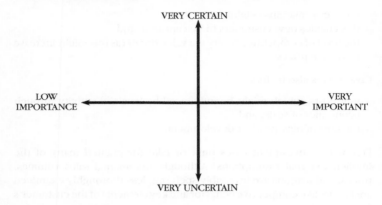

Fig. 4.2 The uncertainty–importance grid.

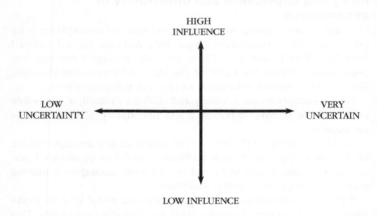

Fig. 4.3 The uncertainty–influence grid.

Exploring the "do-nothing" or base case

Before we leave the topic of assumptions we also need to explore the "do-nothing" or base case option. At Manchester United, for instance, you may need to invest £15mn (net) in new players per annum to guarantee being in the European Champions League (see Chapter 7.)

The "base case" is what might happen without the investment decision. Traditional financial theory teaches us to evaluate incremental cash flows, "incremental" meaning the difference between net cash flows, both with and without the investment project.

A major problem with the base case is that of predicting the rate or pace of decline. This is inherently difficult to predict. Some managers may then try to shield financially suspect projects behind the argument that unless the project is implemented, the strategic and financial health of the business will be irreparably damaged.

Intangibles and interdependencies

Dealing first with intangibles, strategic investment decisions add value only insofar as they are part of the business value system. Interdependencies thus need to be explored because they are essential in understanding how the business operates as a total competitive and financial system.

Interdependencies exist in a variety of forms. Some interdependencies are external and reflect the impact of one external assumption on another. For example, a resurgence of economic growth may increase the size of a particular market and also attract new entrants.

Many of the internal assumptions depend upon external variables, giving rise to even more interdependencies. (For instance, competitive rivalry may lead to a high incidence of price discounting and thus to lower margins.)

But many of the more interesting interdependencies are those within the architecture of the business strategy itself. For instance, one product may benefit or suffer due to the introduction of a new product. FMCG (fast-moving consumer goods) companies realize this, as do supermarket chains opening superstores – these companies are acutely aware of cannibalization effects. But it is not so commonly appreciated in many other industries.

Intangibles are one of the main curses of strategic investment decisions. For many managers, intangibles have become the "no go" zone of financial analysis. Although these are areas of value extremely difficult to quantify in financial terms (and perhaps impossible to quantify with precision), there are invariably ways of defining intangibles better. This can be done by looking at the project from four different perspectives:

» *competitive*: the impact on customer perceptions of value or on measurable improvement vis-à-vis competitors;
» *operational*: performance improvement or flexibility of operations;
» *organizational*: the impact on morale and, indirectly, on motivation; and
» *opportunity generation*: the opportunity that might be opened up or explored as a result of the investment project.

The first step with intangibles is to ask: "Why is the value thought to be of an intangible nature?"

» The benefit may be of a future and essentially contingent nature. It may be contingent because a future state of the world is required to crystallize a market – which may require alignment of a credible product offering, customers recognizing the need exists, and potential demand actually crystallizing.
» The benefit may accrue via a number of internal interdependencies with other areas of the business, or these may occur because the investment project is essentially part of the business infrastructure.
» The benefit may arise due to the project being essentially protective or defensive in nature.

A process for dealing with intangibles is therefore:

» To identify why the value is of an intangible nature.
» To seek possible alternative measures to help target and provide indicators of alternative measures to those of purely financial value.

Defining the business case

When someone says the words "business case" managers often think of a weighty, detailed document with lots of hard facts and financial numbers.

But the real point of a business case is to gain more clarity about the objectives of the project, its implications for the business, and particularly to expose and test the key assumptions which drive value.

This can be achieved in a very succinct way, by for instance restricting the business case to a maximum of eight pages (often less will suffice).

FORMAT FOR A BUSINESS CASE

- » Executive summary (1 page).
- » Project definition, objectives and scope (1 page).
- » How the project adds value (new opportunity, tangible synergy, defensive or protective value) (1 page).
- » Key external and internal assumptions (with an evaluation of importance and uncertainty) (3 pages).
- » Implementation issues (1 page).
- » Summary financials (1 page).

This brings the total length to eight pages plus detailed appendices containing technical details, detailed financial and non-financial measures and milestones, detailed financial sensitivities, detailed resource requirements – possibly another seven pages. This brings a typical case to just 15 pages.

In order to put together a robust business case you should:

- » *be disciplined in data collection*: only collect data which will help you make the critical assumptions which the project depends on (this actually means spending less time on those assumptions which are less critical, such as more minor internal costs); and
- » *not try to obscure or conceal the project's downsides*: an astute review panel will quickly identify issues which you have glossed over.

Business cases will only add value therefore if:

- » they expose the most important and uncertain assumptions, and also address these both in the sensitivity analysis and via contingency planning; and
- » they do not fall into the trap of seeing the financial numbers as absolute measures of value, but use these creatively. For instance, in dealing with less tangible factors it may be fruitful to put an illustrative value on "what these might be worth."

You will need to understand the key value drivers and to expose and challenge the key assumptions *before* undertaking the sensitivity analysis. If you do not, you may just end up with "insensitivity analysis" – playing with the assumptions to get the desired answer: a positive Net Present Value (NPV – which in this case means no more than "Numbers Prevent Vision").

Finally, you need to deal with the terminal value, which is the value which is put on the cash plans at the end of the time horizon of the projections. With slow payback decisions the terminal value can amount to between 40% and 50% of NPV. Yet terminal value may be subject to minimal strategic and financial scrutiny. Invariably, terminal values can be proved more effectively using a quick competitive and financial scenario which, although broad-brush, checks that the assumptions make *prima facie* sense.

CONCLUSION

Strategic investment decisions are at the very heart of shareholder value management. High levels of financial return typically do not occur in commodity industries (for example the oil industry); they occur in industries with complex business value systems (see also Chapter 7 on the Manchester United case), market imperfections and tangible competitive advantages. High returns may be gained through temporary conditions, and lapse or be sustainable.

KEY LEARNING POINTS

» To evaluate a strategic investment decision effectively you need to think through its impact on competitive positioning, the key uncertainties, future alignment both within the business model and outside vis-à-vis its environment, and value and cost drivers.

» NPV is highly sensitive to these external factors.

» The uncertainty–importance grid should be used to help tease out the greatest vulnerabilities, to focus the sensitivity analysis and to generate innovative thinking on how the strategic investment decisions can be improved and made more resilient.

NOTE

1 Mitroff, I.I. & Linstone, H.A. (1993) *The Unbounded Mind*. Oxford University Press, Oxford.

The Global Dimension and Acquisitions

» Financial resources and business assets need to be managed on a global basis.

» Acquisitions are a major vehicle for mobilizing corporate resources to deliver value, but frequently end up destroying rather than creating value.

» The case of BMW's acquisition of Rover is a classic example of how over-enthusiasm, a lack of understanding of the strategic drivers, and misguided implementation can destroy shareholder value.

INTRODUCTION

Shareholder value can be impacted on both positively and negatively by a number of factors which might either enable or constrain globalization. But before we examine these factors we should take a closer look at what globalization really means.

The concept of globalization came to the fore with Bartlett and Ghoshal's book on *Managing Across Borders*.[1] This book argued strongly for creating a more global perspective in the management of businesses. But at the same time it recognized the need to acknowledge how local needs might need to be taken into account when managing across material boundaries.

The slogan "Think Global, Act Local" was born out of these ideas. And we should apply them similarly in the way in which shareholder value is managed.

George Yip, in *Total Global Strategy*[2] took the concept a stage further by examining the extent to which global thinking can be applied to the management process. For instance, one might well establish a common, global brand but then choose to develop human resources on a tailored, and local, basis.

Applying the same line of thinking to the management of shareholder value, we see the various forces emerge (see Table 5.1).

More specifically, perhaps the most impressive area where globalization has impacted on shareholder value is cross-border acquisitions. What better case exemplifies this than the BMW/Rover takeover, which involved stakeholders in the UK (BAe/Rover, and the UK government), in Germany (BMW), and also in Japan (Honda, Rover's previous joint venture partner)?

BMW appeared to be lured into making this acquisition by two concerns:

» the need to become a significantly larger player on the global scene and
» the need to get greater economies of scale.

In 1994 BMW contemplated its first ever major, cross-border acquisition by bidding for Rover Group, then owned by British Aerospace (with a minority stake held by Honda).

Table 5.1 Global/local forces.

	Towards global	Towards local
Product/market exploitation	The more global culture	The continuance of local cultures
Acquisitions	The need for global economies of scale	Local market differentiation inhibits global synergies
Business processes	The drive to accelerate decisions, and facilitate co-operation across boundaries	Remain locally idiosyncratic
Organization	Lean and focused	Traditional culture
Financing and the cost of capital	Global financing – to achieve least cost	Local financing – maximizing flexibility

DETAILED EVALUATION – EXTERNAL

The detailed external analysis of a target focuses on understanding the inherent attractiveness of its markets – and of its competitive position. This can be achieved by using the GE (or General Electric) Grid (see Fig. 5.1)

Originally devised by General Electric, a highly successful US conglomerate, the GE grid answers the questions:

» Which businesses are in the most inherently attractive markets?
» What businesses have the strongest competitive positions?

Ideally, you would wish your businesses (existing and acquisitions) to be in inherently attractive markets and to have very strong competitive positions. Businesses with such positionings are highly likely to be very significant creators of shareholder value.

In using the GE grid we need to go down another level of analysis – by setting criteria for both "inherent market attractiveness," and for "competitive position."

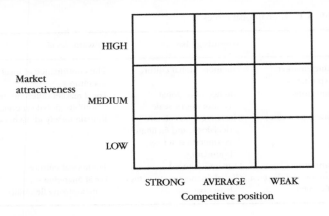

Fig. 5.1 GE grid.

BMW'S STRATEGIC POSITION – 1994

BMW was a very successful company which had exploited important niches in the car market, with a very strong differentiation strategy.

By 1994 (when BMW acquired Rover Group) BMW had built a very impressive position. This brand superiority had been established by very clear market positioning, very high quality product, and service from its dealer network to match. The very success of BMW meant, however, that it had become a prime target for competitors to imitate.

By the mid-1990s there was a very real threat of competitive fade – and thus of reversal of shareholder value creation around that time. In fact, there were a number of symptoms that led to a turning point reached in BMW's strategic health around the early to mid-1990s.

Even before BMW had actively considered buying Rover it had already decided to experiment with the smaller end of medium-sized cars with the BMW Compact, launched in 1994. So at the time BMW *did have* organic options to its acquisitive strategy for Rover Group, which might have been more effective in creating shareholder value than the acquisition of Rover. Summarizing BMW's strategic position as at 1994, therefore, we see that it:

» had been (and still was) a very successful company which had achieved market leadership in the executive, high performance car market in Europe.
» had a worldwide reputation for quality which is now being imitated by a variety of players.
» had a product line which was beginning to appear out of synch with the changing market environment, and one which appeared somewhat limited and perhaps over-focused.

Specific options which BMW might have come up with at the time are:

» to acquire Porsche;
» to acquire Volvo;
» to merge with VW Audi;
» to enter a partnership with VW Audi;
» to set up its own four wheel drive business; and
» to apply its engine technology into other markets (perhaps in boats or public transport).

Having analyzed BMW to explore its options for creating shareholder value, we now turn to Rover Group's strategic position.

ROVER'S STRATEGIC POSITION – 1994

Mrs Thatcher's government sought to sell Rover Group off in the late 1980s following a difficult history in public ownership. BAe then acquired Rover for around £150mn in 1988 from the UK government.

In 1994 Honda had a 20% stake in Rover Group, and this strategic alliance appeared to be working very well. Honda saw Rover as a central plank of its European strategy.

The Honda connection enabled Rover to tap into Honda's technology. The Honda link came at a price, however, as Honda's bargaining power enabled Honda to extract value out of the relationship through its technology licensing arrangement. In the long term, therefore, the Honda partnership began first to dilute shareholder value, and then even to destroy it.

In terms of its products, Rover had previously had a product mishmash, with large executive cars alongside the smaller Maestro, Allegro, Metro, and Mini.

Rover's key competitive weaknesses in 1994 were:

» its relatively small size, and dependence on Honda technology;
» the need for investment on a scale which was difficult to finance through internal cash generation (especially to reposition it on the GE grid); and
» its relatively high unit costs (against other competitors) – due to relatively low economies of scale and to its complex product range.

So, overall, in 1994 Rover had both a fragile competitive position and very slim possibilities indeed of creating sustainable shareholder value. Moreover, outside the UK its brand was weak, its market share was low, and it lacked a strong distribution network.

To get a better idea of Rover's strategic position, let us therefore look at the product/marketing positioning of the Group. To achieve this we will position Rover's products on the General Electric (or GE) grid (which is invaluable for appraising the value potential creation of business strategies). The GE grid maps product/markets in terms of their inherent attractiveness – which is a function of:

» the rate of sustainable market growth; and
» the level of competitive pressure in the industry.

The significance of the positions on the GE (in broad terms) is:

» *North-West*: a very major generator of economic profit.
» *South-West*: a significant generator of economic growth – but with constant struggle.
» *North-East*: a marginal generator of economic profit.
» *due South*: a mixture between just break-even in economic profit and some economic profit dilution.
» *South-East*: a significant if not major zone of shareholder value destruction.

On the horizontal we thus plot relative competitive position, factoring in here Rover's relative value added (to customers) and unit costs relative to competitors.

Figure 5.2 now uses the GE grid (as of 1994) to analyze Rover's product/market niches. The 600 series is shown as being pushed to

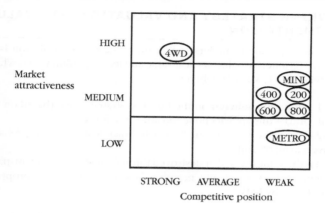

Fig. 5.2 GE grid – Rover Group (1994).

the right due to advancing competitive position. The 800 series is also weakly positioned.

By contrast, the Rover 400 and 200 and Metro niches were (then) in marginally more attractive markets (due to the assumed trend by customers to fewer, smaller cars) although with weak competitive positions. The Metro and Mini are not seen as competitively strong and the Mini in particular is depicted (without new investment) as being dangerously close to the brink.

The overall profile (apart from the four wheel drive which is undisputedly in the North-West), is weak. This cried out for huge new investment which would dilute future shareholder value. And this huge requirement was one of the big factors which blew BMW's integration plans off course. Even with the four wheel drive, competitive rivalry was increasing rapidly.

A substantial part of Rover's current profits were reputed to have been earned by the Discovery alone, so concerns about its future position on the GE grid were important. Clearly BMW was banking on the growth drivers for four wheel drive winning out – as penetration of Europe was only 2.5% (compared to 10% in the US) there was still a belief that growth would win out.

LINKING STRATEGY AND VALUATION (1) – VALUE SEGMENTATION

A crude approach to understanding the value of an acquisition is to analyze its inherent value, its deal value and its integration value (which we will call V1, V2, V3), where:

» V1 is the value inherent in the business strategy itself (based on the GE Grid) – this appears none too attractive for Rover;
» V2 is the value added through the particular deal – this was probably overpayment; and
» V3 is the value created or destroyed through post-acquisition management – this was actually negative, due to perhaps inappropriate strategies by BMW.

V1 can be understood more deeply through the GE grid. But we can also draw up separate lists for the major high-level value drivers and high-level cost drivers, information that was used to understand BMW's acquisition of Rover more effectively. Possible value drivers included:

» four wheel drive;
» executive cars;
» smaller cars;
» latent brands; and
» Honda processes.

Possible cost drivers included:

» replace Honda;
» reposition mainstream cars;
» four wheel drive investment;
» productivity;
» exchange rate; and
» change generally.

Notice in these lists the dependence of Rover Group on the value generation from the four wheel drive Discovery model. Also notice the number of major cost drivers reducing the value generation of Rover.

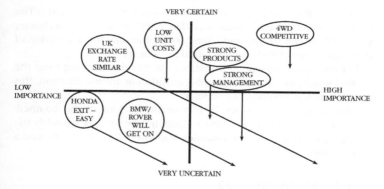

Fig. 5.3 Uncertainty–importance grid – Rover acquisition.

LINKING STRATEGY AND VALUATION (2) – SCENARIOS AND RISK

Figure 5.3 uses the uncertainty–importance grid for BMW's acquisition of Rover Group. This shows BMW's assumptions as follows.

» Rover's existing product range (volume cars) was reasonably strong.
» The four wheel drive Discovery model would remain highly competitive.
» Rover's unit costs were reasonably low.
» Rover's dependency on Honda could be removed without doubling or trebling existing investment levels.
» Rover's existing management resources were "strong".
» BMW would be able to get on well with Rover's management team.
» Sterling would not strengthen by over 20%.

These became both more important and more uncertain, shifting both South and East.

These shifts might have been anticipated before the event.[3] The effect of these adverse shifts was that BMW destroyed shareholder value of between £2.5bn and £3bn.[4] Yet at the time the acquisition of Rover (at around £800mn) was felt to be "cheap."

But with post-acquisition investment in Rover increasing from the £100–150mn per annum level pre-acquisition to around £500mn, this acquisition was anything but "cheap."

This meant big increases in investment to protect the competitiveness of existing models, and to launch new models – notably the smaller, four wheel drive Freelander, the Rover 75, 45 and 25, and a deluxe Mini.

THE DEAL VALUE – V2

The continuing case study of BMW's acquisition of Rover Group in 1994 now illustrates how the process can easily become subservient to the acquirer's drive to consummate the deal. Interestingly, Honda, Rover's (then) alliance partner did not seem prepared for BMW's "surprise" bid, even though the five year period after its initial acquisition expired in 1993. (The UK government, which had sold Rover to BAe, had stipulated that it could not be sold for at least five years.)

That BAe got a good price for Rover Group is undeniable. The *Sunday Times* (August 8, 1993) foresaw (based on informed industry comment) that Rover would be sold for £400–£500mn plus debt, just over half the BMW price tag.

The case study of BMW's deal process in buying Rover highlights a number of key lessons on managing shareholder value.

» The would-be acquirer needs to monitor potential acquisition targets continuously, not only in terms of their performance and potential, but also in terms of the likely enthusiasm and pressure for sale. BMW achieved this very well, but Honda not so well.

» There is an inevitable trade-off between the need to conduct thorough operational due diligence and the need to head off competing bids.

» When there is competition in the frame, it is very easy to overpay for the deal. Whilst a price tag of £800mn on profits of £50mn does not seem extravagant (in price earnings or ratio terms), if the deal had been looked at in more prudent cash flow terms, the huge underlying investment need of Rover would have made it very hard indeed to justify a positive NPV of this order.

But we should also look at the acquisition process itself. How easily and speedily did the acquisition integrate relative to expectations? This is a central question. BMW unfortunately left Rover virtually to manage itself for the first 18 months, and then intervened decisively (and some would say unwisely) in its development, bringing to it its own concept of what "Britishness" meant to the brand.

MORE RECENT DEVELOPMENTS

In early 2000 BMW finally succumbed to the costs of post-acquisition losses at Rover Group. Approached by a venture capital firm Alchemy, BMW agreed a deal to dispose of Rover's loss-making business – with major sweeteners as a pay-off (the four wheel drive business was to be sold to Ford).

Whether by design or by accident, BMW omitted to tell the UK government of its plan. When the news was broken on television the government was absolutely livid that they had been kept in the dark over this deal. UK television was dominated by the news for 48 hours afterwards.

The UK government had just cause to be angry, as they had provided significant investment grants to BMW Rover to help fund new model launches.

The cost of the proposed deal with Alchemy was that BMW fell out of favor with the government, sales of BMWs fell in the UK (BMW's number one export market) and BMW had to pay Alchemy compensation for switching the sale to rival bidders Phoenix.

From the BMW/Rover case, we see that shareholder value can be pursued on a global scale by a number of major routes, namely:

» strategic decisions;
» cross-cultural management;
» global sourcing; and
» global financing.

Strategy decisions

As we saw with BMW and Rover, it is essential to examine the global logic for strategic decision. To what extent does having a global reach actually add to, dilute, or potentially destroy shareholder value? It appeared that BMW felt it needed to be global – but exactly why was this? In reality, any new economies of scale proved elusive, as Rover merely added another and quite complex range of new products on top of BMW's.[1] Also there appeared limited brand-related synergies, especially as BMW did not want its brand tarnished by the variable quality of Rover's (then) products.

Key pointers to genuinely global strategic decisions which might generate shareholder value include:

» globally based economies of scale;
» global brand extension;
» globally spread R&D; and
» global market knowledge and management skills.

Cross-cultural management

Even where global economic change yields potential for increasing shareholder value, this may be frustrated by cultural differences – especially between the managers of country subsidiaries. At BMW/Rover some of the key cultural differences were:

	Rover	BMW
Attitude to project delivery	"More or less on time"	"Precisely on time"
Attitude to problems & communication	"We have a little problem"	"It is not going to happen"
Attitude to quality	"We are trying our best"	"Perfection"

The above differences led to major shareholder value destruction through disruptive reorganization and management changes, delay to the launch of the new Mini, and escalating product development costs, (for instance in the four wheel drive Freelander).

Some routes to overcoming these differences include:

» development of common, world class processes (for example for R&D product development, quality control, and business processes);
» shared management contingencies – to promote a common mind-set and common behaviors; and
» open discussion of culture differences.

Global sourcing

Global sourcing can provide a strong economic rationale for having globally spread or focused operations. By focusing world production on locations which either have particular skills (centers of excellence) or low unit costs, one can manage both global value and cost drivers more effectively. Some key areas to think about include:

» what are the relative (economic) advantages of having plants producing all products required locally versus just a few (or "focused" manufacturing)?
» where are the lowest cost factors of production, and what is the cost of managing any risks of poorer quality?

At BMW/Rover there was only limited scope for reorganizing production on an international basis, reducing the potential for shareholder value creation.

Global financing

Global financing economies are perhaps easier to achieve than the other aspects of global management that we have covered. This is possible particularly through:

» fast remission of cash to a central source – which can then be produced and managed by a centralized, global treasuring unit;
» careful tax planning – to minimize unnecessary tax charges in countries with relatively high tax rates (through transfer pricing etc.) – to the extent that this is ethical/legal;

» raising new capital – by raising capital in the most appropriate markets, minimizing transaction costs and interest costs, and centralized funding of longer-term capital; and

» management of foreign exchange transactions to minimize group exposure to volatile currency movements.

TEN WAYS OF CREATING SHAREHOLDER VALUE ON A GLOBAL BASIS

1 *Markets*: Focus on those markets which have structurally favorable characteristics (higher growth, lower competitive pressure) and where you have real competitive edge. (In Rover's case these were the four wheel drive market in the UK and the US. Markets which were neither structurally favorable nor ones in which Rover had a real competitive edge were the UK fleet market (medium and larger cars) and the UK smaller car market.)

2 *Customers*: Align your organization to focus on the international requirements of customers, rather than on internal needs.

3 *Competition*: Track your competitive position against the varying positions of your competitors across global markets – to assess longer-term market-by-market potential for shareholder value. (Notably Rover's Discovery model might have been "very strong" in the UK but "average" in the US against strong competitors there.)

4 *Brands*: Develop your brands with both a global perspective and with a local perspective. Following BMW's take-over of Rover, BMW intervened to make Rover's cars "British" in what would appear to be an outdated way with little appeal in the UK, Rover's core market.

5 *Products*: Look at the possibilities for globally targeted products (with local tailoring) – to achieve real economies of scale.

6 *Acquisitions*: Consider not merely the more obvious acquisition opportunities (e.g. Rover) but also other ones which might be available globally (e.g. Porsche, Volvo, maybe even Audi/VW).

7 *Alliances*: Seek out alliances where there are: inherently attractive market opportunities; and where your bargaining power will be sufficient to generate shareholder value. (Ultimately, the alliance with Honda diluted or destroyed Rover's shareholder value due to Honda's negotiating power.)

8 *Culture*: Do not assume that consumer or organizational cultures will be similar. For instance, the BMW and Rover cultures were very different, causing tensions and conflicts between the two organizations. This led to value destruction through delays to product launches and increased costs (witness the Mini).

9 *Management*: Define world class management skills and invest in this softer area as this is one of the key longer-term routes to real shareholder value creation.

10 *Finance*: Manage your pool of financial resources (short-, medium-, and longer-term) on a global basis – both to focus investment on the best opportunities, and to take advantage of the best funding sources, and funding economies of scale.

KEY LEARNING POINTS

» Globalization needs to be adjusted to the particular market situation.

» Acquisitions need to be skillfully managed to achieve both global advantage and the creation of shareholder value.

» Acquisitions (like BMW's acquisition of Rover Group) frequently destroy shareholder value owing to:
  » not having explored other options (both organically and other potential acquisitions);
  » not understanding the target's strategic value drivers;
  » overpaying; or
  » integrating poorly or inappropriately.

» The target's strategic value drivers can be best understood using the GE grid.

» Cultural differences can upset cross-border acquisitions and destroy value.

NOTES

1 Bartlett, C.A. & Ghoshal, S. (1989) *Managing Across Borders*. Harvard Business School Press, Boston.

2 Yip, G.S. (1992) *Total Global Strategy*. Prentice Hall, Englewood Cliffs.

3 See Grundy, A.N. (1995) *Breakthrough Strategies for Growth*. Pitman Publishing, London.

4 According to some sources – see for example *The Independent*, March 28, (2001).

The State of the Art

» Strategic value drivers like PEST factors and Porter's five competitive forces shape shareholder value creation to a major extent.
» The cost of capital depends on a company's risk premium and capital structure.
» Financing strategies can be elaborate and esoteric. In the future, there is potential for refinement of approach – seeking to quantify less tangible investment in the business.

THE EXTERNAL MARKETS AND VALUE CREATION

There are many links between external markets and internal value creation. We begin with traditional strategic analysis, covering PEST and Porter's five competitive forces.

PEST factors include the political, economic, social and technological factors impacting on a business externally.

The five competitive forces include:

» buyer power;
» threat of entrants;
» supplier power;
» substitutes; and
» competitive rivalry.

Impact of PEST factors on shareholder value

» *Political*: Regulatory constraints close down opportunities for profitable development.
» *Economic*: Economic cycles either relax competitive conditions artificially or harden them unduly during recession. The impact on shareholder value is to generate volatile sales volumes, prices, and margins – and restructuring costs.
» *Social*: Changes in social attitudes and lifestyles present new expansion opportunities (or opportunities for value added and price increases), or close down suddenly lucrative opportunities
» *Technological*: Technological developments open up new industry structures which encircle and make redundant one's own, or present "leapfrog" opportunities. Technology presents new ways of adding more customer value at the same or less cost, or delivering value quicker, changing the very basis under which competition is possible.

The five competitive forces – and their impact on shareholder value

» *Buyer power*: High bargaining power of buyers increases the costs of maintaining market penetration and customer base. It also increases costs of acquiring customers. It will also reduce the general price level and increase discounting.

» *Supplier power*: High supplier power increases the costs of bought-in goods and services and makes discounts harder to obtain.
» *Entrants, substitutes and competitive rivalry*: These competitive factors magnify the pressure on margins. They also increase the costs of having to continuously improve products and service delivery.

The five competitive forces thus play a profound role in dictating routes to competing successfully – and simultaneously influence the resultant level of returns to shareholders.

FINANCING ADVANTAGE – AND THE CAPITAL MARKETS

Companies obtain capital from both investors and banks to invest in projects and acquisitions carrying varying degrees of risk. These investments are expected to generate returns greater than the returns required by the capital providers. The higher the risk, the higher the return investors require.

We now examine:

» capital market theory and structures; and
» understanding the cost of capital in practice.

Capital market theory and structures

Shareholder value takes a different perspective to that of conventional financial accounting through its emphasis – perhaps obsession – with cash flows.

The virtue of cash flow is that it represents a truer measure of the economic value of a business than short-term, backward-looking profitability measures.

Economic value is arrived at by adjusting the future value of cash flows to their present value equivalent, and then deducting the initial investment to arrive at a Net Present Value (NPV).

Also, by targeting for positive Net Present Values we can ensure that business projects generate just enough economic profit to pay the investors the rates of return they require, given the project's risk.

But how do we arrive at the cost of capital? This is achieved by understanding first the risk-free rate of return and then the additional risk premium for "equity" or risk capital.

The risk-free rate of return

The costs of capital to a company are a combination of the costs of its risk capital or "equity," and also of its debt.

The market cost of equity

To calculate the market cost of equity, we first estimate the risk-free rate of return, and then add the extra return over and above the risk-free rate that is required by equity investors (i.e. the "equity risk premium").

The risk-free rate of return is the return required by investors where they are not exposed to any risk. This is defined as shown in the following equation:

rate of return on an equity = risk free rate

+ risk premium on the equity

The weighted average cost of capital (or WACC) is then calculated. The weighted average cost of capital takes into account the cost of equity, the cost of debt, and the proportions of debt and equity in the capital structure as a whole.

The WACC is the basis of the hurdle rate used by companies when deciding on new investments and is also useful in valuing existing business strategies, too. The funds provided by investors are expected to return on average at least the weighted average cost of capital. For those managers with a more technical inclination the relevant equation here is:

The weighted average cost of capital, or WACC, is calculated as shown in the following equation:

WACC = (rate of return on debt after tax

× debt as a proportion of capital)

+ (rate of return on equity

× equity as a proportion of capital)

Debt as a proportion of total capital should ideally be calculated using the market values of both debt and equity (and not the balance sheet values of debt and equity which are historic).

To think about this in personal terms, consider a person with a £100,000 mortgage (with interest at 5%) and with bank loans of £20,000 at 15%. An equivalent, weighted average cost of borrowing would be:

» £100,000 × 5% = £5000 per annum of interest
» £20,000 × 15% = £3000 per annum of interest
» totals £120,000 = £8000 per annum of interest

So the weighted average cost of borrowing would be:

» £8,000 on £120,000 = 6.66%

Illustration: understanding the cost of capital in practice

Whilst there may be an overall cost of capital for a group, where there is a conglomerate, different cost of capital may be appropriate to different businesses, as we shall see. For instance, consider the following conglomerate group with three divisions consisting of leisure, property, and retail.

Given the projected past tax cash flows of the business, the profiles shown in Table 6.1 emerge.

Table 6.1   Sector profiles.

	Leisure	Property	Retail
Annual turnover of each division	£350mn	£70mn	£280mn
Divisional cost of capital	12%	14%	13%
Present value of cash flows	£58mn	(£2mn)	£7mn

Here, although the property division is relatively small (10% of group turnover of £700mn), it destroys shareholder value. Retail is only just breaking even, whilst leisure is the powerhouse of shareholder value. This analysis might suggest that the property division is a candidate for turnaround or disposal. Parts of the retail division may also need similar treatment.

FINANCING STRATEGIES

One of the key challenges of shareholder value management is to source finance at an optimal cost. In our previous section we looked at the need to understand and manage the cost of capital. We now give you some checklists which will help you to think through optional financing strategies. Run through these in your own mind for your business.

Working capital

» Can debtors be managed more effectively to reduce future working capital requirements (e.g. through credit terms)?
» Is factoring of debt an economic way of financing working capital?
» Can stock levels be managed better – for example through just-in-time systems?
» Is the company's gearing (its value of debt to equity) either excessively conservative or too liberal?
» Does the company have the most appropriate mix of shorter- and longer-term debt to fund expansion?
» Are their innovative sources of debt or similar forms of capital which could facilitate expansion or reduce costs of capture?

Other financing

» Would franchising enable the business to expand more rapidly and easily?
» Is off-balance-sheet finance an appropriate way of funding the business?
» Are joint ventures (and collaborative arrangement generally) an appropriate path of:
  » strategy development; and
  » of helping funding?

» Should the company invest directly in its assets (including property), or is leasing a better approach?

Managing shareholder perceptions

» How attractive is the business to new forms or sources of finance (including private stakeholders, venture capitalists, etc.)?
» If the company had considerably more money to fund growth, what kinds of opportunities (and returns) could be addressed?
» How secure is the earnings (and thus the cash stream) of the company – both in reality and as perceived by investors?

Future financing

» What is the company now worth (to a potential buyer), and is investment an attractive possibility (either now or in future)?
» How (and when) might the company be floated and what changes would it have to make to prepare for this?
» Does the company have sufficient financial reserves (cash and borrowing power, and potential capital issues) to seize attractive acquisition opportunities?

Strategic considerations

» Are margins sufficient to generate the external funding for growth – given the assumed capital intensity of the business?
» What is the most appropriate level of dividends (and growth path for dividends), given future expansion plans?
» How might potential changes in the mind-set of financiers towards this particular industry affect our ability to expand (as in 2000, during the collapse in dot-com company shares)?

Regardless of the strength of your current operating cash flows, it might be both useful or essential to raise finance externally to develop and protect your business, and to grow.

Table 6.2 compares and contrasts some of the specific pros and cons of particular sources of finance.

The criteria for choosing a source of finance include:

1 sufficiency (does it give enough finance and over a sufficient length of time);

Table 6.2 Merits and demerits of sources of finance.

Sources of finance	Pros	Cons
Operating profits/cash flow	Comes without ties (once dividends are well covered)	Expensive capital and might be constrained
Overdrafts	Cheaper (relatively)	In theory, can be called in
Longer-term loans	Alleviates shorter-term liquidity pressures	Secured on assets – and might be constrained (and increases gearing)
Private investors	Often cheaper, more flexible than other sources	May come with personal agendas and obligations
Venture capitalists	Finances riskier ventures	Very expensive and risks loss of control
Share issues	Reduces gearing	High transaction costs – and expensive

2 flexibility;
3 cost (relative to substitutes);
4 risk; and
5 acceptability to stakeholders – including investors and managers.

Financing choices can be made using the Financing Option Grid (see Fig. 6.1), where each box is completed as follows:

» *three ticks*: very attractive;
» *two ticks*: medium attractiveness;
» *one tick*: low attractiveness.

The rest of this section deals with some of the main ways of sourcing finance. This is slightly technical so readers who are more interested in the principles of financing than the details should feel free to skim or skip.

CRITERIA	OPTION 1	OPTION 2	OPTION 3
SUFFICIENCY			
FLEXIBILITY			
COST			
RISK			
ACCEPTABILITY TO STAKEHOLDERS			

Fig. 6.1   Financing option grid.

Companies can also look to specialist financial instruments to help supply finance, and these are quickly summarized. They include:

» trade debtor management – including factoring;
» international sources of debt (e.g. the Euro-securities market);
» syndicated loans (these being loans from a consortium of banks, and other financing sources);
» mezzanine finance and junk bonds, which are loans whose conditions put lenders at relatively high risk, but which command higher than average returns; and
» derivatives including forward tracking, futures, options, and swaps.

In particular, factoring involves title to debts being vested in a finance house, which pays the company on initial sale, and then makes a charge (often significant) for providing funding in between sale and receipt of the cash.

The Euro-securities market enables a company to tap into other financing markets by raising debt in other currencies. Whilst this may be cheaper it is also risky, as you will then be exposed to adverse currency swings.

Syndicated loans are a way of several lenders minimizing their exposure to a very large amount of finance – especially where the company's credit rating is less than wonderful.

Mezzanine finance is unsecured debt (or preference shares) which offer high returns at high risks (often the premium is 2–5%). Such debt is issued when borrowing limits are reached and the firm cannot or will not issue more equity.

Bonds with these characteristics are usually called junk bonds, which became very popular between the mid-1980s and mid-1990s. Their high return is matched by high risk.

A derivative is an asset whose performance is based on the behavior of the value of an underlying asset (for example, a commodity or foreign exchange currencies). Derivatives give either the right or the obligation to buy or sell a quantity of this underlying asset. Derivative instruments include futures, options, swaps, and forwards.

The important things to bear in mind here with sources of financing (over and above their technical complexity) are:

» To what extent do they actually minimize costs?
» If they do minimize costs, do they achieve this without pushing up risks unduly?
» What might go wrong to make a risky position into one of potentially huge exposure (for example general crises in financial markets)?
» To what extent will innovation in this area make investors nervous about the financial stewardship of the organization?
» What is the total degree of financing risk – aggregating separate balance sheet and other sources – across the company?

To complete our review of sources of financing, it would be remiss not to mention how risk and uncertainty impact on shareholder value management, particularly in applying the cost of capital.

» *Risk analysis using probability scores and weightings*: Although this is easy to illustrate mathematically, most managers are not attracted to heavily quantitative and statistical measures.

» *Analyzing the component of business-related risk within the cost of capital*: This is reflected in the discounting principle (using NPVs or Net Present Values).
» *Uncertainty analysis*: This can be addressed through scenario development (telling stories about the future).
» *Default risk*: This is the risk that the company cannot comply with the contractual terms of a financing deal (whether this is a loan, a foreign exchange futures contract, or an exposed position in a derivatives market). Default risk is a function of:
  » economic volatility in the general environment (in the economy or financial markets);
  » the company's cash flow;
  » the inherent riskiness of the financing instrument(s); and
  » the financial exposure to this financing generally.

A LOOK TO THE FUTURE – LIKELY TRENDS AND DEVELOPMENTS

As we look to the future, a number of potentially interesting developments lie ahead, including:

» more sophisticated integration of strategic and financial analysis in the management of shareholder value;
» further development of "option theory" (see Chapter 8) as a vehicle for appraising strategic options' economic value in both uncertain and contingent conditions;
» more work on how to appraise the economic value of intangibles. For instance, it would be particularly useful to develop ways of putting an economic value on brand investment. Also, past developments in putting a value on strategic thinking[1] could be developed further;
» putting a value on protective value – particularly to address heading off major uncertainties – would be extremely useful; and
» further thought on how to apply managing for value at a more micro level.

Focusing on the last point (which merits further expansion), shareholder value can be most useful when managing specific micro-level projects (which are likely to dilute, and possibly even destroy share-holder value).[2] Moreover, managing for value can be useful to address key questions at an individual level, namely:

» How do I currently add economic value within the organization?
» How *could* I add economic value to the organization (in future)?
» Which organization could I (personally) add most value to?
» How can I add more economic value on a basis?

We may also need to consider how you (as a manager) add value over time, either in operational projects or to track value added within specific meetings. At Hewlett Packard, for example, one senior director took this idea on board and used it to pinpoint three key value-creating modes:

» I am adding value (a "green" card);
» I am uncertain whether I am adding value (a "yellow" card); and
» I am probably, if not certainly, not adding shareholder value (a "red" card).

By using this color-coding system for managing meetings and memos she was able to cut out the 20% of her time which was value-destroying.

KEY LEARNING POINTS

» Porter's five forces and PEST factors have a profound – if some-times indirect – impact on shareholder value.
» Economic value is the net present value of free cash flows.
» Free cash flows are discounted by the cost of capital, which is usually based on the weighted average cost of capital.
» The cost of equity is the risk-free rate plus the risk premium on that particular company's shares, depending upon the industry it is in.
» A wide variety of financing strategies are available to minimize the cost of capital.
» Further developments are likely to come from option theory, from valuing less tangible resources and investment decisions,

from valuing measures to protect shareholder value, and from applying value-based management at an everyday level.

NOTES

1 Grundy, A.N. & Brown, L. (2001) *Be Your Own Strategy Consultant*. International Thomson Publishing, London.
2 Grundy & Brown, *ibid.*

Shareholder Value – Success Stories

» The BP Amoco case highlights that shareholder value needs to become top management's central concern and that its implementation can take a number of years to realize its full benefits.
» The IDV case suggests that managing for value yields important insights about business issues and choices, typically changing resource allocation. But again, it requires considerable culture shift.
» The Manchester United case illustrates the impact of value migration in generating superior shareholder value, and the impact of life cycle effects – past, present, and future.

In this chapter we focus on three key success stories showing how shareholder value has been implemented. The first case study is that of BP Amoco, one of the world's very biggest oil companies. The second is International Distillers and Vintners (or IDV) – part of Diageo group. The final one is Manchester United and the football industry which is an example where, implicitly, shareholder value has been a major vehicle for corporate development – and not just in the UK, or Europe, but globally.

SHAREHOLDER VALUE – BP AMOCO

This case study follows the argument already spelt out – that strategy and value are complementary perspectives on business management. We have already seen in preceding chapters that many of the problems associated with making corporate investment decisions are attributable to an unnecessary schizophrenia between strategic and financial appraisal. In this chapter we explore how "value-based management" has contributed to making corporate investment decisions to maximize shareholder value within BP Amoco.

This account of value-based management at BP is explored as follows:

» background to value-based management at BP;
» evolution of the process; and
» reflections on the BP experience.

Background to value-based management at BP

Although no one will need reminding that BP is an oil company, by the early 1980s BP Group had diversified into a number of areas including chemicals, coal, gas, minerals, and nutritions. This diversification strategy led to increasing difficulty in allocating investment resource between the various divisions of BP. A large central corporate planning department assisted BP's senior executives in making corporate investment decisions from head office but this advisory task was progressively transferred to the international business in line with a policy towards decentralization.

In common with many other large groups, BP's corporate strategy then experienced a major shift in the mid-1980s. Sir Peter Walters, then chairman, began a program of refocusing BP's corporate portfolio in order to concentrate on BP Group's core competences which were in oil and closely related businesses. In a series of disposals and acquisitions, BP rebalanced its portfolio of businesses to once again concentrate primarily on the oil business, but retaining businesses with clear and tangible synergies – principally chemicals. This rebalancing included the disposal of mineral activities to RTZ, and the acquisition of Britoil and the remaining 50% stake in the Sohio associate company. BP's nutritions division was all that remained as an indirectly related business – but the strategic logic here was the very strong competitive position which BP had built up by a sequence of well-managed acquisitions.

Arguably, therefore, the task of making corporate investment decisions in BP should have been made much simpler by these developments at corporate level. But problems of evaluating corporate investment decisions within a strategic *and* financial framework remained. The process of simplifying the "businesses BP is in" had highlighted some important residual problems. These were concerned with linking these decisions with BP's corporate planning process, its control process, and ultimately with its rewards systems.

Evolution of the process

The evolution of value-based management (VBM) at BP can be split into four separate phases:

1 diagnosing – the "performance measurement review;"
2 piloting VBM;
3 implementation – VBM planning processes;
4 implementation – VBM control and rewards systems.

Diagnosis

The diagnosis phase began when top management at BP initiated a major review entitled a "performance measurement review." This grew out of concerns about the relevance of "Return on Capital Employed" (ROCE) as a measure of corporate and business performance.

BP's managers felt uncomfortable with ROCE for several main reasons.

» ROCE is based on financial accounting measures. These measures do not necessarily reflect how successful the business is in generating shareholder value.

» ROCE is backward- rather than forward-looking: it measures past and recent performance rather than the business's capability of generating future cash flows.

» Whilst BP's managers were asked to make decisions on the basis of future cash flows, paradoxically they were judged and rewarded on the basis of performance measures which were accounting-based and historic.

When the performance measurement review team first reported back the practical problems caused by using ROCE, they also identified an approach called "value management" which the team felt "might be worth taking a look at."

Top management at BP felt that this idea of "value" offered further promise. Even though there was relatively little precedent for this approach in the UK, it was felt that the matter was worth exploring further. BP began the next phase of the study by working together with a US firm of consultants (Marakon) with experience of VBM to explore its potential for BP.

The consultants were given the following brief. First, to have a "quick look" at what BP's corporate portfolio might be worth in terms of NPV of the projected results of existing business strategies. Second, to take a more "in-depth" look at some *specific* areas of BP where value was being created or lost.

Piloting VBM

The second pilot phase of this exercise was an eye-opener for both BP management and the consultants, even though both parties were sophisticated in their use of strategic and financial planning techniques. There were a number of early insights.

» Some (though not all) of BP's newer activities created less value than had previously been believed. For example, in one case it was revealed that BP's competitive advantage in a market not closely related to its core businesses was lacking.

» Through examining BP's value chain under a microscope, it was found that whereas in most cases the picture of where shareholder value was created matched previous BP thinking, in a number of notable areas it did not. This raised some key strategic questions about some business areas. These not only concerned their competitive position and market attractiveness but also whether they represented value-creating opportunities sufficiently large to be worth pursuing.

The consultants faced a steep learning curve as they grappled with the specific problems posed by BP's strategy, structure, and finances. Particularly contentious was that of BP's corporate cost of capital. Although both BP and the consultants agreed on the appropriate rate to use, there was some technical debate as to how to arrive at that rate. This may seem, at first sight, to be an academic issue as both sides agreed on the actual rate to use. However, this was not simply academic as potential changes in BP's mix of businesses, financial structure, and perception by the stock market might well result subsequently in the two approaches giving significantly different answers.

Some of the key insights from this second phase of development of VBM were:

» that VBM is not a "magic tool" or black box which will answer all planning and control difficulties at a stroke – it needs to be applied and tailored intelligently to its specific context;
» that applying VBM is an ongoing learning process – not only about how value is generated or lost in the business but also about how to use the tools themselves; and
» any company thinking of applying VBM should avoid overselling the process; expectations also need to be carefully managed, particularly concerning the lead time to implementation.

The pilot phase thus established VBM as being the core framework for corporate planning and corporate investment decision-making in BP Group. The "pilot" enabled the infrastructure to be set in place for the roll-out into planning processes throughout the BP Group.

VBM planning processes

During the third phase of development of VBM, the process was successively and successfully applied in BP's international businesses.

This roll-out was co-ordinated by BP's internal team, who worked hand in hand with BP's business managers in their ongoing planning and decision-making processes.

According to the (then) project leader of the team, Simon Woolley:

> "Where you applied VBM, there were always surprises. For example, I was sitting with one BP manager and we were looking at a model of his business which represented his future profitability and cash flows from operations and key assumptions about the market. The manager explained that it was easy to generate additional value through business growth as profitability was increased.
>
> "But we then played a 'what-if' scenario which increased the growth rate of part of the business using a cash flow model of the business's operations. The manager was shocked when the NPV of the business strategy actually went down. This was because the 'growth' was not 'profitable growth' in value-based terms: although it was apparently profitable on an accounting basis, once an allowance for the time value of money had been made and particularly adjustment for additional working capital, it was not. This taught us a lot about the business as it not only raised questions about incremental value creation but also about the quality of opportunity facing this business and its competitive position."

Simon Woolley then goes on to describe how managers found the use of VBM during this key phase:

> "At first managers appeared to expect absolute answers to an imprecise problem – measuring value creation. As they learnt more about VBM they began to realize that the value of VBM lies not so much in absolute measurement but in its power of making comparisons.
>
> "For example, VBM really comes into its own when comparing major strategic decisions or options for a particular decision. It is also useful for comparing different financing options – which I would stress again is a separate issue to evaluating the strategic opportunity itself.

"Obviously it also enables you to post-audit your decision after the event. Finally it enables you to benchmark your performance relative to your competition.

"If I might expand on the latter point, we are now at the point where we don't simply say, 'What a great performance last quarter' – just because the oil price has leapt up. We compare our performance not just against what we said we expected to achieve but also against how specific competitors have done in the same or similar environment."

The strong impression gained from this account is that implementation of VBM is something which does not happen overnight but is a gradual process involving sustained learning and continual effort. Recognizing the need to share this learning, Simon Woolley set up a "corporate network" for debating VBM within BP Group. This network is a meeting of practitioners of VBM across BP businesses which meet off-site to debate and agree "best practice" VBM methods and to spread the "VBM message."

VBM control and rewards systems

Phase 4, which was implementing a full VBM control and rewards system, was then commenced. Only recently have the first full year's plans under VBM been monitored and controlled. Again, this has provoked healthy debate concerning what factors might have been "controllable" versus those which were "uncontrollable." VBM therefore involves not merely *measurement* but also the ability to interpret these measures against a background of change. Because of this, VBM should not be applied through exact and rigid controls, but should be sensitive to external context and also tolerant of areas of unavoidable measurement error.

By the stage of implementation, VBM needed to become *the* language of planning control and rewards systems. The latter issue is of considerable interest as management behavior is unlikely to change materially.

The application of VBM-based rewards systems does, however, raise further issues which needed to be addressed at BP. Although a lot of work had been done to link top managers' rewards to shareholder value at BP Group level which was benchmarked externally, difficulties still remained at senior and middle levels of management. Further work was then needed to link these rewards to value generation at the business level. For functional heads it was found possible to target and measure performance against specific value and cost drivers. A framework of "critical success factors" (see also Chapter 2) is then established for optimizing value and cost drivers so that managers can be targeted on achievement against these factors. This recognizes that manager(s) should be rewarded for how they succeed in controlling these levers which drive value in the business. Thus the focus is away from being purely an historic performance which mixes controllable versus uncontrollable factors together.

This phase of the process was perhaps the most difficult of all as it most directly affected managers individually. As VBM is not an exact "scientific tool," rewards systems need to be set up which capture broad measures of performance rather than exact levels of achievement.

Key insights on the BP Amoco experience

BP Amoco's experience of VBM over the past years raises a number of broader lessons about linking strategic and financial appraisal, about the role this can play in the management process, and about how change of this kind can be implemented.

First, BP Amoco's experience reveals that VBM can bring together a variety of key elements in the management process, including:

» strategic and financial planning at corporate and business levels;
» corporate investment decisions, including organic investment, acquisitions, and divestments;
» evaluating revenue expenditure programs;
» corporate finance, dividend policy, investor relations, treasury management, financing decisions, and tax planning; and
» performance targeting and measurement and rewards systems.

The following summarizes critical success factors which might enable implementation of VBM:

» top management being visibly committed to, and actively interested in, VBM;

» "value" to shareholders being set alongside ambitions to satisfy other corporate values. It should not be seen as the *sole* objective of the organization (unless that is what the "corporate mission" says);
» VBM embracing planning, control, *and* rewards systems;
» managers being trained to use cash-based financial tools (DCF) *and* being exposed to strategic analysis tools;
» willingness to explore areas where value may not be currently optimized;
» early handover of management of the process to management – rather than having it championed by external consultants;
» having a clear plan early on for a roll-out program throughout the organization; and
» managing expectations so that managers will realize that the lags will occur between investing in change and reaping the rewards.

On the other hand, there are a number of areas to avoid in implementation of VBM. First, there is a danger that VBM could degenerate into a "number crunching" exercise where financial modeling takes on a life of its own. Second, one can fall into the trap of playing the "VBM game" through manipulating terminal values of business strategies – these need to be tested against external assumptions rather than added on simply as a notional multiple of earnings. Third, VBM should not be applied only to a particular area of the management process or business – for example, solely to capital investment decisions or to core operations but not to newer business areas. Finally, it is sometimes tempting to accept compromise in order to make headway – for example, deciding to defer indefinitely any changes in rewards systems during the roll-out program.

In summary, here are some of the key benefits which have come out of the migration to VBM.

» BP Amoco now has a common framework for integrating long-range strategic plans, capital programs, acquisitions and divestment business cases, and short-term budgets.
» This is also being married to its rewards systems so that behavior and motivation are aligned to decision and control processes.
» In specific areas of its operation, BP Amoco decided either to divest or refocus its businesses.

» VBM is now applied increasingly to test value-generated major elements of cost in its revenue budgets.

» There has also been a realization that a trade-off not only exists between large investment projects but also between value generated by these and by revenue cost programs.

» Some notable "prizes" have been won through using VBM to make better financing decisions, with direct and measurable impact on shareholder value at corporate level.

» Finally, performance management at BP Amoco has become much more outward-focused and geared to achievements relative to competitors and also relative to market conditions.

STRATEGIC FINANCIAL MANAGEMENT AT INTERNATIONAL DISTILLERS AND VINTNERS (IDV)

Introduction

As we saw at BP Amoco, managing for shareholder value is a philosophy rather than a quick fix. Introducing it to an organization requires sensitivity to the organizational culture and controls, and to its key stakeholders – and their perceptions, their power base and fears. The IDV case study shows not only that implementing shareholder value management can be highly attractive, but that it can also be relatively difficult – unless these factors are thoroughly understood.

Implementing shareholder value management at IDV

IDV is a major international subsidiary of a top 10 plc; it is global in focus with a UK head office. Its portfolio includes a large number of consumer brands marketed and sold on a worldwide basis.

This case illustration brings out the many practical issues which need to be dealt with in implementing shareholder value management, highlighting the problems of managing shareholder value at a practical level, and especially how to make the transition from old to new ways of doing things. In effect, IDV was trying to change its controls, its routines, and its management rituals to create a shift in its management style. We also look at some of the key implementation issues which shareholder value management faced.

The shareholder value management process began at IDV with the perception that a value gap existed between currently projected value creation and corporate and divisional financial targets. These targets reflected shareholder aspirations. IDV then performed a review of business areas. This review established the extent to which these businesses currently created, diluted, or destroyed value. It also examined their potential to create value in the future.

This phase led to a more detailed examination of increasing investment or decreasing investment options. A particular issue was the need to reduce product complexity – in particular, parts of worldwide distribution. In addition, IDV needed to consider the country/market priorities and strategic options associated with these.

In parallel, the corporate and divisional financial targets influenced plans (along with views on longer-term investment/divestment). But equally important were the external pressures facing the managers of the business units.

Besides these internal and external influences on business plans, corporate rewards and mind-set also had a pervasive role. As we will see, it took some time before these softer factors began to realign and facilitate value-led change in both operations and management.

The key implementation themes in the IDV case are:

» increasing investment;
» reducing investment;
» dealing with product complexity;
» country participation; and
» managing shareholder value as culture change.

Increasing investment

A senior finance director (then at IDV) explained some of the benefits of the process, particularly when reviewing extra product investment.

"We did a lot of work on a major product in the USA, with the marketeers playing a central role to evaluate the effects of changing our advertising spend to secure more shareholder value.

"This change in strategy is working well. Because we put in extra advertising we were able to increase the price. We are seeing quite significant improvement in performance.

"This investment had been pretty successful both financially and in building brand equity. People felt that it showed we were committed over time, and that they would be protected. Although in certain circumstances, because of the focus on getting year-end figures, we have actually cut expenditure which created a credibility issue.

"The managers said: 'You mean you still expect us to deliver all your longer-term financial targets. But you reduce our current investment simply to achieve our short-term financial targets.'"

Expectations about what shareholder value will lead to in the way of resource reallocation thus play an important role in determining whether it will be incorporated as a management process or rejected with cynicism.

Reducing investment

Besides highlighting products to increase investment, shareholder value may also identify products to reduce investment.

"People often believe that if we find a negative economic profit (in a particular business area) then this inevitably means an exit strategy.

"For instance, one particular product was a value destroyer. But what you may have noticed is that it hasn't been on the television for the past two years. We couldn't justify the advertising investment that we were incurring on television to stimulate extra volume and margin. So we have taken that spend away. This has helped to move profitability in the direction of value creation even though it still consumes value and ironically volume has not significantly declined."

In conclusion, although a product may be destroying value currently, there may still be options for retaining it, for example by reducing the level of ongoing investment.

Dealing with product complexity

Shareholder value can play a major role in re-engineering and simplifying the business strategy. The finance director continues:

"We are far more ruthless now with new brand development. We are cutting out things which fail. We may say, yes, we can tolerate that brand for the next three years destroying value, but you do recognize that it is this much this year, and it is this much next year, and after that we expect it to come through and add positive value."

The goal of simplification becomes more difficult because of problems with justifying reduced profit contribution.

"But the real difficulty is to say, 'What is the incremental effect, for example, of taking just one brand out?' Our view might be that we can sell a brand for a certain amount of money, but everybody else then says, 'What about the rest of the portfolio, it doesn't do anything for us.' But actually it does, it clutters up the system, all of your stock, our stock turnover ratios, it does all of those things and there is no simple way of analyzing the cost.

"For example, we have a sales force that sells three major products (and many minor ones). If we reduce our range of brands we have to consider what we do with the overheads that are left over."

He then takes a step back from this to reflect on the bigger implications for the brand portfolio.

"It is also linked to the question of size of brand portfolio. We have got so many brands – we have a lot of secondary brands now – it is cluttering the portfolio. But there is a reluctance to take them out because they are generating contribution.

"If you take all the major products in our portfolio, and if you look at a certain product, without question it would improve the quality of the portfolio, but would it really mean that you would get extra margin?"

So, in conclusion, simplifying the product portfolio is frequently an essential – although tricky – part of beginning to bridge the gap between destroying value and beginning to add value (or the "value gap").

Country participation

In addition to product-based decisions, IDV also had to understand country participation issues. The finance director explores this as follows:

> "With one non-core product where we weren't putting in any investment at all but which was important in some countries, we found it was destroying a lot of shareholder value.
>
> "But we found a local company who required additional capacity, so they got benefits out of it. We were then able to keep the distribution in the two key markets which we wanted, and we only lost a small amount of contribution. We got rid of all the assets, all the problems of manufacture, and we retained our distribution where we wanted it, and sub-contracted production of two other brands at reduced costs. So that was a great deal – there were benefits to us and there were benefits to them. This was really a two plus two equals five.
>
> "In one country we have reduced our overheads whilst retaining our market position. In another country we have said we are not going to be here on the ground but we are going to give our brands to a distributor. So we have proactively reduced value destruction without jeopardizing our brand's market position."

Obviously, where a company has a matrix of product and country markets, this adds an additional dimension to shareholder value management. Here we need to look at both the implications of options across markets (for a product) and options across products (for a particular country market).

Shareholder value management as culture change

The finance director recognized that linking strategy and value inevitably meant a major change in management culture – and it was therefore not just a project with a particular end point.

> "One of the major difficulties that we had was the perception that this was a project, and that it is not a fundamental behavior change. IDV is great at central initiatives where you go away

and you persuade people that something new is important. And because of that decision people saw the process as a one-off.''

Shareholder value management had a considerable impact over both local and group lever power structures:

> "The big lesson, if we wanted to do it more quickly, was that the holding company had to buy in. We weren't managing the interface which said 'earnings' were more important than value – and that was a big, big lesson."

In summary, the corporate culture is thus a major factor which will facilitate or constrain the application of shareholder value management. It can take considerable time and persistence to achieve sufficient change in understanding and behavior to bring about value-led change.

> "Prior to shareholder value, people's objectives were market share, and that maximized operating profit – that's not value creation. For example, when making an acquisition, previously managers in businesses around IDV would have signed a bit of paper about how much of the new brands acquired they would sell. But when you go back to the post-acquisition and say 'Hey, how are the brands doing?' they would say 'Well, you know, I am being told to concentrate on my core brands, therefore this brand is deprived of financial and people resource.'"

In conclusion, linking strategy and value (through shareholder value management) is part of a particular management culture rather than being simply a bundling of analytical management techniques that give us a "better answer."

Key insights from IDV

Despite these problems, IDV management have made some major breakthroughs in managing shareholder value employing the shareholder value management philosophy. This has been achieved despite the complexity of dealing with a number of implementation themes of increasing investment, decreasing investment, dealing with product complexity and country participation.

The key insights from this process (as from earlier documented cases such as at BP Amoco, where it took almost five years to achieve the full benefits) are that shareholder value management needs the complete and sustained backing of corporate management from the top down in order to be successful. Shareholder value management, if implemented partially and without deep commitment, will only deliver limited benefits.

But shareholder value management is one of the essential ways of making strategic management a reality – particularly in stretching managers' vision from the short term. And after three years it is being adopted by IDV as the key process in managing the organization. The full benefits of shareholder value management at IDV would not have been realized had shareholder value management been considered merely an overhaul of "how we do the plans and our numbers around here." Real strategic decisions at the corporate and business level and a change in management mind-set need to occur for "managing for value" to realize its full value.

Final conclusion

Managing for value is a process which integrates a diversity of techniques. These techniques cover strategic analysis and economic analysis.

Virtually every major company's annual report and accounts today espouses the need to manage for *shareholder value* and is dotted with references to "strategy." But whilst managers may see the imperatives of value-based management, they may well not feel confident about *how* to implement it. The IDV case study highlights that these issues must be faced up to.

MANCHESTER UNITED AND THE ASSOCIATION FOOTBALL INDUSTRY

The football industry is one which has traditionally added value in simple ways but which has changed into one that is complex, changing the basis of competing and of shareholder value creation. It is thus an excellent case study in value migration.

The industry context

Association football ("soccer") is the most popular spectator sport in Britain, with six times more attendance than the next most popular sports – greyhound racing and horse racing. Football is also received with similar enthusiasm in many European countries – and indeed worldwide, where frequently the level of excitement generated exceeds that in the UK.

To understand some of the external value drivers in the football industry we will draw on Porter's five competitive forces of:

» bargaining power of the buyers;
» bargaining power of suppliers;
» threat of substitutes;
» rivalry; and
» threat of entrants.[1]

Applying Porter's five forces analysis to the football industry, we can make the following summaries.

» Buyers have a relatively low bargaining power (as their loyalty to clubs in traditional customer segments is usually very high). This loyalty is now breaking down as an increasing proportion of followers watch different teams. This force historically supports above-normal value creation in the industry, but this effect may disappear.
» Suppliers do have considerable (high) bargaining power – these suppliers being particularly the players. Players' salaries absorb typically over half of gate takings and high-performing players command considerable transfer fees. This force may thus undermine value creation in the industry.
» Substitutes are an important threat. We include here direct substitutes such as other leisure activities, besides indirect substitutes, such as watching games on satellite television. This force thus poses a growing threat to value creation.
» Oddly, there is not typically an intense rivalry for fans on a local basis, although rivalry on the pitch is high. The "rivalry" force does not act to depress industry profits in a serious way. This force thus plays a neutral or even positive role in supporting value creation.

» Entry barriers are very high both to the industry and also between groups of clubs – especially for those aspiring to be major clubs.

This competitive forces analysis suggests that, although the competitive environment generally supports a super-normal value creation in the industry, as most of these forces are favorable, there are significant longer-term threats to this. Recent growth trends may be largely responsible for investors seeing this industry as generally "attractive" (i.e. offering superior returns) and as offering future potential of further value generation through pay-per-view televised matches. Let us take a closer look at how these "super-normal" profits are distributed in the industry.

Surprisingly, perhaps, the football industry has traditionally not been a very profitable one overall. In 1993–94, for instance, during a time of recession, English professional football as an entire industry reported a pre-tax profit of just £12,000 on turnover of £387mn.

The strongest group of the Premier League clubs (known sometimes in strategic management as a "strategic group") have exploited – and some would say over-exploited – their merchandising.

This phenomenon in turn raises some issues about the sustainability of the cash flows arising as a result of the merchandising strategies of clubs like Manchester United. If it is no longer so trendy to be seen walking around with Manchester United's latest replica strip (which changes periodically), this could pose a major threat to both the volumes and margins of merchandising operations. (In 1996, Verdict reported that the football merchandising market stood at £150mn, or approximately 3.7 million strips per annum at an average price of £40, suggesting near market saturation.)

Football has therefore developed from its traditional base of taking receipts for the game to a much more complex set of business activities, for example sponsorship, advertising, television, merchandising, conferences, and catering, extending its value domain. Potential future value-creating activities include the Internet and also mobile telephones.

To summarize, football has been transformed from an industry with relatively low value creation to one with high value creation – for Premier League clubs. By changing the way in which value has been created in the industry, Manchester United has achieved extraordinary returns for its shareholders.

Manchester United and shareholder value

Manchester United has been a very successful football club for several decades. It has thrived despite setbacks – for example, the Munich air crash around 30 years ago which effectively wiped out the team. In the 1960s it spawned players like Bobby Charlton and George Best, and under Alex Ferguson, its manager, has rekindled this success in the 1990s.

Manchester United has been instrumental in changing the game from being primarily a spectator activity to a mass, market-based product. This has transformed its financial results.

Financial analysis of the breakdown of the club's turnover during the early 1990s highlights how the industry – and in particular Manchester United – changed its ability to generate value dramatically. The revenue of Manchester United has grown rapidly since 1989: all categories of revenue have grown but that from merchandising has increased the greatest – with a decrease in the proportion of revenue coming from gate receipts. By 1995 Manchester United's profits stood at a staggering £20mn, dwarfing Glasgow Rangers' £7.1mn, Barcelona's £8.5mn, and Real Madrid's £3mn.

Value-creating activities

First of all we look at:

» Value creation in the football industry – and at Manchester United
» Value creating activities
» Value drivers
» Cost drivers
» Shareholder value – a future scenario
» Lessons on future shareholder value creation.

Value creation in the industry – and at Manchester United

Shareholder value is created in any business through the interaction of a number of external and internal factors which we call the "business value system." Besides the traditional value-creating activities of fans paying to see their team in action, the years 1994 to 1997 saw a huge growth in football merchandising.

This merchandising includes, for instance, Manchester United replica strips which cost anything between £30 and £45 for children, and up to over £60 for adult strips.

A business value system for the successful football clubs is shown in Fig. 7.1. This highlights the need to maintain match performance as a means of providing the platform for value-creating activities elsewhere. It is precisely because of the interdependencies within this business value system that you cannot naively answer the question of creating activities elsewhere.

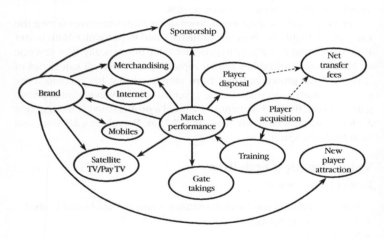

Fig. 7.1 Business value system – football clubs.

Value-creating activities

This question is also linked to the adjacent one of: "Where (and how) will we make money in the future?"

Although this is a question implicit in most treatments of strategy formulation, in practice this question is very much at the forefront of managers' minds.

For example, if we focus once again on Manchester United, some very major pressures on its drive towards game commercialization have emerged. A backlash has emerged from sections of the traditional fan base, who have actually demanded seats on the board of Manchester United.

Media coverage is likely to prove an increasingly important source of revenue. Manchester United has already set up its own Sky satellite channel. Also, revenues from European matches are expected to increase considerably. This was a major factor that increased the club's market capitalization to a healthy £0.5bn by late 1996.

A summary of how Manchester United as an organization now adds value (and potentially destroys value), and to whom, (thus incorporating an under stakeholder perspective) can be found in Table 7.1. This highlights the tensions that might arise in managing the club, for example between:

Table 7.1 Value creation and destruction factors. Note: "value creation" means either positive cash flows or the creation of other, less tangible, value to the shareholder.

Stakeholders	Value added	Value destroyed
Fans	Hard to get in (tickets are rationed) – making it a special experience	Merchandising costs
Players	High salaries Transfer fees	None
Managers	Salaries Profit sharing	None
Merchandisers	Sales of kit	None
Media	Media revenues	Falls in media revenues
Shareholders' dividends/profits	Share price rises	Share price falls

» the interests of players (in securing high salaries) versus managers and shareholders (profits);

» the interests of media versus the club in dividing up television and satellite revenues; and

» the interests of management and shareholders in balancing shorter-term profits against longer-term shareholder value.

Value drivers

Value is created in any business through the interaction of a number of external and internal factors. These combine to generate cash flow either directly or indirectly. At Manchester United an obvious ingredient is the ability to win match after match, or to come back after setbacks, which it has done by winning the Premiership championship year after year.

Whilst media incomes were not crucial by the late 1990s, they were not the pot of gold that one might have expected earlier. The media companies have managed to exert quite strong buyer power and negotiated relatively favorable contracts. The future of football broadcasting will obviously have a very big impact on the business value system of the various clubs. However, in mid-2000 a review of these arrangements has brought even more economic value to the industry and the football clubs are getting a good share of this. This led to their much increased revenue through 2001–2004. Following the fall-off in advertising revenues in late 2001 and the disappointing revenues of ITV Sport, there is a very big question mark about the potential for further longer-term increases in shareholder value, which led to widespread press speculation in November 2001 on the possibility of the creation of a second Premiership League (value migration thus continues).

Returning to the issue of commercialization of the clubs, especially merchandising, it is hard to see how the leading clubs can enhance their existing earnings streams (except in new media revenues – for example, through pay-per-view television).

The merchandising life cycle may however be shorter than imagined since the target market is relatively discrete. It is estimated that at Newcastle United, for example, another club that has been extremely successful at developing merchandising activities, some 75% of their regular attenders at matches now own a Newcastle strip.

Focusing now on the key macro-level value drivers of Manchester United, we see that they fall into a number of interrelated clusters. These consist of:

» merchandising;
» media;
» match takings; and
» effectiveness of play.

Cost drivers

In the 1990s there has been an undeniably increasing pressure on clubs' costs. The transfer market, for example, has grown fast. In 1994–95 £110mn was spent on player transfers (compared with £73mn in 1992–93). By 2000, players were regularly changing hands for over £10mn – and without being wonderful. This represents the working of a constrained factor of production causing asset prices to build up to the point where shareholder value creation is more normalized.

This trend is continuing as top clubs compete more for "big signings" and a higher premium must be paid for star quality. The growing transfer market has also more importantly sparked wage rises and the recent transfer ruling allowing greater freedom of movement for players will accelerate this trend as clubs compete for players with wages. Players' earnings rose by around 20% in the mid-1990s and by 30% towards the late 1990s/early 2000.

By mid-2000, in the wake of the Euro 2000 competition, the market for world class players found itself at new heights. Portugal's player, Figo, was poached from Barcelona by arch-rivals Real Madrid for £41mn (leaving the English player Steve McManaman playing in the reserves for £60,000 a week!).

Real Madrid then bought Zidane for almost £50mn, adding to Real Madrid's mammoth debt. Unfortunately, as a free-roving player Zidane's presence contributed to Real Madrid being halfway down the league table in November 2001.

In parallel with these changes, major investments have been made to grounds and have consumed capital. Continued investments will need to be made but there is a danger that certain clubs will "feel richer" and fuel the transfer market further. Perhaps, at some stage, the bubble will burst even with revenues fuelled by pay-per-view TV – especially as these revenues have not met expectations.

Shareholder value – a future scenario

We now briefly describe a scenario where pressure mounts on football clubs. This impacts significantly on shareholder value. The clubs then revise or moderate their "commercialization" strategy and are left with falling revenues and margins at a time of unduly high costs. The likely result: fall-out of weaker clubs (and maybe even financial failure of one or more of the larger clubs) is a scenario with at least some plausibility. The "endgame" here would be literally restructuring the game. Indeed, the *Sunday Times* (as long ago as 11 February 1996) highlighted one possible new development – a super six-a-side league with the very top players, shorter pitches and even a six-a-side world club competition (a "new industry").

Lessons on value creation – from Manchester United

Manchester United's market capitalization during this period grew considerably, peaking temporarily at £1bn around 2000. This was on the back of its creation of new value-creating activities (over and above gate takings and core TV revenues). Not only did United help transform value creation in the industry generally, it also achieved a very strong competitive position. The reward from these two factors was felt in major shareholder value creation.

In the late 1990s its market capitalization was distorted by two things:

1 BSkyB, the media company, sought to acquire Manchester United for £63mn; and
2 in 1999–2001, hype over the Internet pushed Manchester United's market capitalization to an amazing £1bn.

Although its market capitalization has fallen significantly since 1999 (to around £350mn), due to the Internet Bubble its capitalization still exceeds that of all of the other UK premier clubs combined.

With its rivals hot on its heels, Manchester United felt under pressure to sustain the success of recent years, especially with disappointing results on the pitch in October–November 2001. (These related to an imbalance in the team following expensive new player acquisitions, a confidence crisis generally, and Sir Alex Ferguson's pending departure.)

The key insights from this case study on managing for shareholder value at Manchester United are as follows.

» It is impossible to fully appreciate the factors driving an industry – both now and future – without an appreciation of both the strategic drivers and how economic value is being created in the business value system.

» In order to identify the possibilities for value migration, work backwards from current and latent customer value. What are the distinctive areas of customer value which might cause a customer to re-evaluate perceived value? And how can a reasonable element of this extra perceived value be captured by the company (for example, through a higher price)?

» Besides asking the question, "Where should we go strategically?" you have to ask – simultaneously – "Where and how will we be making money?" The notion that economic value analysis "brings up the rear" – and only follows on from strategic analysis – is a most dangerous and misleading one.

» Effective co-ordination of strategic and financial performance requires skilful balancing and trade-offs, rather than a pursuit of particular financial goals to the exclusion of goals with a more indirect impact.

» Superior shareholder value creation is very much contingent upon creating and preserving an external competitive environment which is conducive to making good returns. This value-generation potential is then amplified by competitive dominance (as at Manchester United), and is then underpinned by layer upon layer of reinforcing competitive advantage. But it is also contingent upon implementing the strategy with effective implementation (or put plainly, "getting it absolutely right"); this does play a very major role in determining shareholder value creation in not only this, but in most other industries too.

NOTE

1 Porter, M. (1980) *Competitive Strategy: Techniques for Analyzing Industries and Competitors*. The Free Press, Macmillan, New York.

Key Concepts and Thinkers

» The first wave of writers included Rappaport, Reimann, Bennett Stewart, Copeland *et al.* and McTaggart *et al.*
» These early thinkers concentrated principally on financial economics and on quantification, with the exceptions of Reimann and McTaggart *et al.*, who took a more balanced approach.
» More recent writers have explored a number of different ways of calculating the cost of capital, and the importance of "real option" theory.

G. Bennett Stewart: *The Quest for Value*[1]

Bennett Stewart's book is a land-mark text, promoting Economic Value Added (EVA) as a central target and measure for shareholder value. His book begins with a discussion of "free cash flow" (i.e. operating cash flow less the annual investment required to sustain those cash flows). Bennett Stewart is one of the founding partners of the consulting firm of Stern Stewart and Co. Again he debunks the idea that account profit is a viable measure of corporate performance, and equally earnings growth.

In an important chapter on "The EVA Financial Management System" he takes us, step-by-step, through the concepts of:

» net operating profit after tax
» the EVA equation (covered in Chapter 2).

This leads on to a discussion of how the cost of capital is calculated, with worked numerical examples for companies such as Wal-Mart.

He then turns to the conditions for generating shareholder value through acquisition, and particularly acquisition pricing, with discussions of the stand-alone value, the synergy value, and the premium value of an acquisition. The use of free cash flow is then looked at within the context of business planning, together with corporate determinants of corporate risk.

Black, Wright & Bachman: *In Search of Shareholder Value*[2]

Black *et al.*'s book is a comprehensive, accessible, and thoughtful account of both the theory and practice of shareholder value management. Beginning with a clear definition of the cost of capital (including how to calculate the Weighted Average Cost of Capital, or WACC), it argues that shareholder value management is not a fad, but a fundamental process. It holds that whilst profit is opinion, cash is fact. It also reconciles the pursuit of shareholder value goals with those of satisfying a range of other stakeholders.

Moving onto technical areas, it explains the role of Betas (which measure the volatility of returns of a particular company relative to the rest of the stock market) in defining the cost of capital.

He then clearly explains Rappaport's key value drivers of:

» sales growth;
» cash profit margin;
» cash tax;
» fixed assets;
» working capital;
» cost of equity;
» cost of debt; and
» capital structure;

as well as the two key measures of:

» economic profit, or Economic Value Added (EVA) – which are in effect the same thing; and
» cash flow return on investment (i.e. the discounted value of the cash flows of the future strategy).

The book then turns usefully to explore the impact of shareholder value on acquisitions, and also explores how shareholder value creation differs by industry type.

Copeland, Koller & Murrin: *Valuation: Measuring and Managing the Value of Companies*[3]

Copeland *et al.*'s classic text is a comprehensive resource for both the theory and the techniques of managing shareholder value. Again beginning with the premise that "cash is king," it starts from the management of shareholder value at the corporate level.

They ask: to what extent can you manage the value of the value of your business better than other people (as does G. Bennett Stewart)? Shareholder value, they contend, can be managed by making internal improvements to the business, or by restructuring these to retain only those parts of the corporate portfolio which it can add value to, either organically or perhaps by further acquisition. Included in this argument is the need to estimate the potential break-up value of the group as compared with the share price.

Once again the book proposes discounted cash flow as being the best model to capture shareholder value, stressing that reported accounting earnings are frequently not well correlated with share price movements.

Through numerous worked examples it shows how to apply the discounted cash flow approach to evaluating the present value of future business operations – it also stresses the need to separate the value of operations in place and also the value estimates of growth opportunities.

A key insight is the need to challenge assumptions about the *sustainability* of the rates of return which are likely to flow out of future operations. This requires an analysis of industry trends and changes in competitive structure and their impact on shareholder value.

The way in which the weighted average cost of capital is estimated is fully explained, along with the adjustments to arrive at a target capital structure for future investment. (This may differ from the present capital structure.) Specific issues such as how to deal with complex capital structures such as swaps and esoteric financial instruments are also covered.

Particularly useful is the book's advice on the alternative formula used for dealing with the problem of "terminal value," i.e. what value to put into the final part of the forecast time horizon. Two options are:

» to a forecast for a very long period, and then assume no value after this; and
» to assume that cash flow will continue indefinitely.

Ellis & Williams: *Corporate Strategy and Financial Analysis*[4]

This book makes a unique contribution to our understanding of historic shareholder value creation. Unlike most of the other texts we have surveyed, it actually begins with corporate goals, capability and position – and links these to the generation of shareholder value. Early case studies include the European biscuit industry and United Biscuits, and also Granada plc. This makes direct linkages with published financial reports and accounts.

It moves on to the link between shareholder value and the shareholder value gap – which is the gap between likely future shareholder value creation and that expected by the shareholders, or aspired to by management.

It then examines the extent to which shareholder value analysis can be applied to historic financial statements. It then compares and contrasts the utility of the profit and loss accounts and the balance sheet with the cash flow statement – the latter in their view is often more significant and informative.

Traditional financial ratio analysis is then examined – particularly in terms of the extent to which these ratios can be used to shed light upon the potential for shareholder value generation. This is then placed in a comparative context, particularly through comparative ratio analysis.

Haspeslagh & Jemison: *Managing Acquisitions*[5]

Haspeslagh and Jemison give us an excellent overview of why acquisitions often destroy rather than create shareholder value. First of all, many management teams are not all that clear on what their acquisition strategy is – both in terms of its purpose, and also for its strategic logic (i.e. how precisely an acquisition will add).

According to Haspeslagh and Jemison, acquisitions can add value either by opening up the business to new "competitive domains" (or marketplaces), or by protecting existing domains, or by generating some real and very tangible synergies. Equally, acquisitions frequently destroy value either through paying too high a premium price or through ill-thought-through integration.

Overpayment itself is often driven by early and premature over-commitment to the specific acquisition. Acquisitions are often made as a means to develop the group but the question of whether there are other routes to develop which might generate superior shareholder value is not often asked. Frequently, companies are acquired with weaker competitive positions, or ones in domains which are very competitive and which are likely to dilute or even destroy shareholder value. To help managers to avoid these, there are some very helpful and comprehensive checklists which can be readily incorporated into your management process.

McTaggart, Kontes, & Mankins: *The Value Imperative*[6]

The Value Imperative is one of the very few accounts of shareholder value which balances the financial and the strategic perspectives evenly.

The Value Imperative describes the process of "Value-Based Management" or "VBM" which, it contends, should be the primary process for managing strategy development, corporate planning and decision-making, and corporate performance management, measurement, and control.

They define VBM as "a formal, or systematic approach to managing companies to achieve the objective of maximizing wealth creation and shareholder value over time." VBM is also a set of beliefs, principles, and processes. The authors are well aware that VBM involves a profound cultural shift. (See also the BP Amoco and IDV case studies in Chapter 7.)

Following a review of the influence of the stock market on shareholder value, they go on to describe the key determinants of shareholder value. They suggest that:

» value is created over time only where a business unit can earn a return which exceeds the cost of its equity capital; and
» growth can be both good and bad: bad growth magnifies value destruction. (Bad growth here being growth into competitive markets or ones where we lack a real competitive advantage.) (See also Chapter 10.)

Value creation depends on either:

1 positioning in market structures which offer more favorable returns; or
2 having competitive advantage which crystallizes in either higher than average prices, or in lower than average costs.

Superior returns can come from either:

1 "strategic assets" – which represent tangible or intangible proprietary assets or knowledge; or
2 "organizational capability" – which represents having superior skills.

These are called "Strategic Value Drivers" by the authors. Every company needs to develop strategies for developing its cost advantage *and* its strategic asset base. Also, the company's strategy needs to reflect whether the company's longer-term interest is best served by developing a high market share through moderate prices or whether it would be more beneficial to generate superior margins through premium prices.

Pricing to capture market share with moderate prices is likely to be more appropriate where:

» there is high market growth;
» there is high operating leverage (and low capacity utilization) or many economies of scale; and
» competitors are slow or unable to react to attacks on their market share.

Pricing for higher margin returns (as opposed to trying to capture market share) would be more advisable where the business is characterized by:

» currently low returns (at or below the cost of capital);
» low market growth;
» low operating leverage and few economies of scale;
» high current market share; and
» competitors who are likely to react quickly to attacks on their market share positions.

The authors then look at how value creation and capital is likely to differ when dealing with entry versus exit strategies.

At the corporate level the strategic value drivers are likely to be shared across at least some business units. This helps support the group's corporate logic – thus bearing the rationale of *these* particular business units belonging to *this particular* corporate group – and not to any other.

The role of the corporate center can also be targeted and valued by looking at the extent to which the group delivers efficient and value added services to the business unit (for example due to economies of scale). These services include: strategic input, treasury, HR development, alliance management, etc.

Moving on, another important insight is contained in the authors' central principle that: "Companies fund strategies, and not projects." In other words, it is held to be a far superior approach to appraise a set of investment projects at the business level rather than a particular project as a discrete set of incremental cash flows. This is because of the complex effect of interdependencies between strategies and projects.

Also the authors contend that conventional capital budgeting processes are notoriously vulnerable to manipulation by smart managers, who can easily get the "right answer" and produce a positive NPV by diligent use of spreadsheets. In essence, therefore, they view the value of a business strategy as being the sum of existing and new investment projects.

Madden: *Cash Flow Return on Investment (CFROI Valuation)*[7]

Madden's book is an exhaustive account of modern cash flow based methods of valuing a business.

It begins with clear linkages between shareholder value and four key business variables:

» growth;
» skill (managerial);
» competition; and
» operational performance.

Madden's treatment of "management skills" is useful and interesting. He lists the following as being important:

» vision and strategy;
» alignment (both internal and external);
» feedback, learning and innovation;
» maintaining organizational adaptability; and
» ability to transmit knowledge internally, and to turn it into value.

Madden's core argument is that conventional valuations of future cash streams are backward-looking. Conventional estimations of the cost of capital are based on *historic* trends, as exemplified by the Capital Asset Pricing Model (or CAPM). Madden suggests that the cost of capital should be calculated by looking forward – to estimate as an alternative future returns and then relate these back to current valuations (by shareholders).

In effect, Madden's CFROI is defined as being the internal rate of return at which future cash flows reward investors sufficiently to put their money into the company – based on current share prices.

Put very simply:

Current valuation = Present value of cash streams from *existing*

assets + Present value of *future* investments

To arrive at the present value of cash streams from existing assets Madden needs to estimate:

» the lifetime of existing assets (which is done by working out how long assets are likely to last based on their current net book values and their depreciation rates); and
» projections of the interim cash flows, including the investment required to sustain the business.

This means in effect, that you need to look forward to anticipate a company's life cycle CFROI, given its competitive position and the characteristics of the industry. In fact, Madden also devotes considerable space to the analysis of historic CFROI. This suggests that many companies go through periods of significant shareholder creation, then of shareholder value dilution, and subsequently move into a phase of shareholder value destruction. His interesting graphs of some real-life case studies compare and contrast the creation/destruction of shareholder value with the growth in real assets of the company (these grow even into the value destruction phase).

The second part of Madden's valuation equation – the present value of future investments, poses greater challenges. It might be relatively easy to predict a "reinvestment rate" of positive cash returns (as he does) and perhaps the effectiveness of management skills. However, it is harder to predict the future opportunity stream and the concept of the rate of "competitive fade" – which occurs due to competitor catch-up, customer learning, and technological advances generally.

Even the notion of "management skill" might not be as solid and stable as might have been thought. For example, the collapse of Marconi (formerly GEC) in 2001 which led to write-offs of over £5bn under the auspices of Lord Simpson and John Mayo (its finance director) was spectacular. When the new management (who had replaced Lord Weinstock, who managed the old GEC conglomerate in a financially conservative manner) took Marconi aggressively into telecommunications their, vision and strategy, learning capability, and ability to align operations with their environment may now seem suspect.

Clearly, Madden's model is likely to prove more difficult to apply in highly volatile markets, and ones where value is very much focused on very novel opportunity streams, and which are highly dependent upon the high level of management skill.

Depending upon the time horizons for estimating value, Madden's model will have a varying level of significance. Madden's calculations reveal that CFROI for US companies in 1997 was 7.5% (the long-term historical average was just 6.0%). This means that investors were looking towards higher returns in the future than those which had been achieved in the past.

For some industries (with shorter asset levels and investment time horizons), this minor difference in discount rate of 1.5% would not be highly significant. But for investments in longer-term cash streams such as in industries like natural resources, petrochemicals, utilities, transport infrastructure, and aero-engines, the effects would be considerable.

To calculate the present value of cash streams from existing assets Madden estimates:

» the current values of existing assets (as if this is new and today's investment decision). This is based on their balance sheet values;
» projected sustainable cash flows; and
» a final terminal value (if any) in relation to any worth of the business once its physical assets have expired.

In order to calculate the current value of balance sheet assets, Madden works through a whole chapter of extensive adjustments, for example to arrive at the current costs of inventory and to adjust the value of intangibles.

Certainly this is a "state of the art" approach, but a slight doubt remains that where the non-quantitative imponderables are very substantial – as in the brief Marconi example – there might be some risk of working very hard at calculations when more qualitative factors might be equally, if not even more, important and fundamental.

But of course the latter point applies to all theories in shareholder value – we need to avoid being "precisely wrong," and perhaps try to be more "approximately right" in considering shareholder value creation and its measurement.

Mills: *Strategic Value Analysis*[8]

Mills' book is another, more financially based, technical account of economic value analysis. It gives a good treatment of evaluating strategic investment decisions, following Rappaport's value driver structure for its business valuation,.

It gives a particularly useful account of ratio analysis – for example in looking at Market to Book Value, which compares a company's estimated market value with the historic cost (suitably depreciated) of its net assets. This analysis can suggest either over- or under-valuation of a group.

Mills also deals well with estimating the cost of capital, with acquisition evaluation, and with some suggestions on the integration of shareholder value analysis within the management process.

Morin & Jarrell: *Driving Shareholder Value*[9]

Morin and Jarrell's impressive book is an answer to the need for a "how to" book which links strategy and value, portfolio management, competitive strategy, operational excellence, business process management, core competencies, and management incentives. As Morin and Jarrell point out, despite the considerable literature on shareholder value (covered above), it seems odd that institutional investors still focus on dividend yield and growth, upon quarterly earnings per share, and managers seem still not to fully understand NPV.

In essence, their book integrates

» strategy
» finance; and
» corporate governance

in a single, holistic framework. Initially they follow the conventional framework of putting forward return, growth, capital, and risk as being the four key determinants of shareholder value. Like Rappaport and Reimann before them, they trace value creation back to market economics and to underlying competitive position. Whilst market economics is traced back to the political, economic, social and technological (or "PEST") factors – and to Porter's five competitive forces, this seems to omit frameworks to incorporate growth, such as growth drivers.[10]

One of their real and leading contributions is that of "Real Options Theory," which offers some very interesting insights on the economic value of maintaining flexibility. According to Morin and Jarrell, "real options" refers to "management ability to adopt and later revise corporate investment decisions in response to unexpected and risky market developments."

Shank & Govindarajan: *Strategic Cost Management*[11]

Cost is a very key issue in shareholder value management, as it is one of the key areas of resource allocation (and equally of misallocation). Cost should be managed to trade off long-term against short-term needs, and internal efficiency against external competitive effectiveness.

Shank and Govindarajan give us a comprehensive (if complex) overview of how to manage costs in such a way as to add to shareholder value, as opposed to undermining it. For them, strategic cost management requires value chain analysis (which also links to the idea of "business design" (see Slywotzky below), to strategic positioning, and to cost-driven analysis).

Cost drivers are split into "structural" cost drivers. These include: industry economies of scale; business scope; the effects of the experience curve (how well the company has learnt to get its costs down); and its technology base.

Alongside the structural cost drivers we also see that "executional" cost drivers are important too. "Executional" cost drivers are concerned with how well that area of cost is managed on an ongoing basis. The central tenet of strategic cost management is that costs are not well managed in the conventional, one-year, budget process as this:

» tends to spread resources too thinly, diluting shareholder value;
» reflects past patterns of resource deployment, rather than current or future; and
» neglects the longer-term trade-off between short and long term.

In the remainder of their book they explore each area of structural cost drivers, and how to analyze them and manage them.

Shank and Govindarajan's approach moves significantly beyond activity-based costing (ABC), which analyzes costs in terms of cost-behavior and the underlying process drivers within the *existing* business model. By questioning the relevance of the existing business model (as does Slywotzky), we move beyond existing resource deployment and then existing activities.

Slywotzky: *Value Migration*[12]

Value migration can be defined as "moving away from old outmoded business designs to others that are better designed to maximize both customer value and shareholder value." Slywotzky's achievement here is to link in the market value (or capitalization) of companies with their underlying business models.

Slywotzky distinguishes between three simple phases of corporate development and shareholder value:

» *value inflow*: where cost flows are far in excess of the cost of capital due to having a superior and appropriate business model;
» *value stability*: where returns are more moderate, due to increased competitive or customer pressure, or both; and
» *value outflow*: where returns are inadequate, leading to pressure to shift resources into new value-creating activities.

Value migration can occur at an industry level due to new technology or forms of distribution like e-commerce can be initiated by new entrants, or at the business level.

Slywotzky's book is replete with interesting case studies like South West Airlines (a low cost carrier), the pharmaceutical industry, the coffee industry (Starbucks), and the computing industry (IBM and Microsoft).

He then turns to some practical tips on how to anticipate and respond to value migration at an industry level by using scenario-based techniques.

This book is notable for its lack of explicit and detailed financial theory and formulae, but is very powerful in terms of its challenging, qualitative thinking on shareholder value creation.

Ward: *Corporate Financial Strategy*[13]

Keith Ward's book focuses on the interrelationships between the capital market and the competitive marketplace. He traces these linkages through product life cycles, and by relating the market life cycle with how risky a firm's projects are typically perceived to be, and the appropriate financing strategy.

He then turns to classic methods of evaluating the value of the equity investment, including dividend growth models, cash flow based evaluation, and classic earnings per share and assets backing methods.

Whilst financial theory assumes that capital markets operate perfectly, Ward highlights a number of sources of imperfection, particularly those of lack of important information and investors not being perfectly rational in their decision-making. Clearly such imperfections blur the usefulness of market-based measures like share price for making judgements on shareholder value creation (at least in the short- and medium-term).

Moving back into the more recognizable world of investment in real businesses, Ward looks at the role of venture capital, giving a treatment of returns using probability weightings and expected (but not certain), not present, values. There is an extensive discussion of why having a zero dividend pay-out can be appropriate in certain such instances – as reinvestment within the business of cash generated can yield a high rate of return.

Next we look at the slightly more mature but still growing business, and the implications of making rights issues where further capital is raised directly from existing shareholders – who can choose to take up or forgo this opportunity. A rights issue is typically cheaper (in terms of transaction costs) than a public placing of shares open to anyone.

As we move into maturity, corporate dividend policy and the company's dividend pay-out versus re-investment ratio come more to the fore. Ward shows how in a decline situation a higher dividend payout is more attractive and appropriate (although this may be resisted by managers, whose "agency role" – in looking after the value of shareholders – can become submerged under their collection of personal agendas). Another vehicle for enriching the return of shareholders here is to reduce capital through a share buy-back. This is followed by a further chapter on options for the declining businesses.

Finally, the latter section of his book covers innovative financing methods to get the best trade-off between lowering the cost of capital and also financial risk through financing instruments like convertibles.

NOTES

1 Bennett Stewart, G. (1991) *The Quest for Value – The EVA Management Guide*. Harperbusiness, New York.

2 Black, A., Wright, P. & Bachman, J. (1998) *In Search of Shareholder Value – Managing the Drivers of Performance*. Financial Times Publishing, London.

3 Copeland, T., Koller, T. & Murrin, J. (1990) *Valuation: Measuring and Managing the Value of Companies*. John Wiley & Sons, New York.

4 Ellis, J. & Williams, D. (1993) *Corporate Strategy and Financial Analysis*. Pitman Publishing, London.

5 Haspeslagh, P.C. & Jemison, D.B. (1991) *Managing Acquisitions*. The Free Press, Macmillan, New York.

6 McTaggart, J.M., Kontes, P.W. & Mankins, M.C. (1994) *The Value Imperative*. Free Press, Macmillan, New York.

7 Madden, B.J. (1999) *Cash Flow Return on Investment. (CFROI Valuation)*. Butterworth-Heinemann, Oxford.

8 Mills, R. (1994) *Strategic Value Analysis*. Mars Business Associates, 62 Kingsmead, Lechlade, UK.

9 Morin, R.A. & Jarrell, S.L. (2001) *Driving Shareholder Value*. McGraw Hill, New York.

10 See Grundy, A.N. (1995) *Breakthrough Strategies for Growth*. Pitman Publishing, London.

11 Shank, J.K. & Govindarajan, V. (1993) *Strategic Cost Management*. The Free Press, Macmillan.

12 Slywotzky, A.J. (1996) *Value Migration*. Harvard Business School Press, Boston.

13 Ward, K. (1993) *Corporate Financial Strategy*. Butterworth-Heinemann, Oxford.

Resources

There are numerous sources of data about companies' performance in generating shareholder value in the US, in Europe, and more specifically in the UK (for example, London Business School).

Chapter 8 contains an overview of the major books which have advanced thinking about shareholder value over the last 15 years. This chapter focuses more on other sources of data or insights on shareholder value. In the US there are a number of sources of data on shareholder value topics, including:

» *Standard & Poor's Stock Reports*: continuing financial information, current activities, and market segmentation;
» *Standard & Poor's Industry Reports*: containing discussions of industry trends and analysis of specific companies;
» *SEC filings*: containing detailed financial information on specific companies;
» *Moody's manuals*: containing historical financials, with breakdowns of societies and bond ratings;
» *Wall Street Transcript*: containing summaries of analysts' reports and CEO speeches; and
» *Dun & Bradstreet*: contains details of divisions, product lines, and subsidiaries (by industry) of key groups.

More specifically, the Value Line Investment Survey analyzes shareholder value creation for around 1700 companies.

Also, in the US there are computer-based sources of information including Datatext (which contains data on 10,000 publicly quoted companies). An alternative is Dialog, which contains a raft of computerized data including financials, phone prices, ratios, analyst reports, financial abstracts, and an idea of news summaries.

The Dow Jones also publishes stock market prices, dividends and shareholdings, and analyst reports.

Outside the US:

» BARRA International produces individual company statistics – for example, the *World Book* (2500 companies from the *Financial Times* list) – and separate books on:
  » the UK;
  » Japan;
  » Germany;
  » Australia; and
  » certain other countries.

» London Business School has a share price database and a risk measurement service. This helps provide data on betas (contact London Business School, Sussex Place, Regent's Park, London NW1 4SA, England).

» Erasmus University, Rotterdam, Holland contains betas for Belgium, Denmark, France, Germany, Holland, Italy, Sweden, Switzerland, and the UK.

» Karlsruhe University, Germany has very complete German data (contact Institut für Entscheidungs-theorie und Unternehmensforschung, Universität Karlsruhe, Postfach 69 80, D-76128, Karlsruhe 1, Germany).

» Compass contains all significant UK companies and major Euro Companies.

» Datastream is a source for all UK quoted companies.

» Extel contains first year summaries for UK quoted (and major unquoted) companies, including capital transactions, acquisitions, disposals, and dividends.

» M&A Database gives useful data on UK M&A transactions and some US deals.

Stern Stewart of New York also publish a ranking of 1000 companies in the US according to shareholder value creation. Another performance ranking can be found (in the US) in the HOLT J Dual grade performance Score card, produced by Holt Value Associates.

How to Avoid Destroying Shareholder Value: Ten Easy Ways

There are 10 key ways of destroying shareholder value: mission statements, going for growth, acquisitions, investment business, creeping business complexity, cost management, poor leadership, and corporate learning. Each one of these areas needs skillful management to avoid management decisions and behaviors which will destroy shareholder value.

The ten key areas where shareholder value can be destroyed include:

1 mission- and objectives-driven strategy;
2 creeping business complexity in services;
3 tactical pricing;
4 business investment decisions;
5 acquisitions;
6 cost management;
7 change management;
8 product, brand, and technology development;
9 over-commitment, strategic and financial; and
10 denial of corporate error.

Shareholder value is a concept which many companies espouse, but few actually manage on a day-to-day basis. Managers seem to be adept at not creating shareholder value. This chapter focuses on 10 easy ways for them to avoid destroying shareholder value.

1. MISSION- AND OBJECTIVES-DRIVEN STRATEGY

Although many writers extol the benefits of having a mission, this can easily misdirect management. Invariably, the mission is stretching and may often be unrealistic, yet it may still exert a powerful influence over strategic and more tactical thinking.

In order to avoid a mission- and objectives-driven strategy, the following measures are needed:

» an analysis of the organization's internal capabilities *before* formulating the mission.
» trying to work upwards to a mission, based on a thoroughly analyzed competitive strategy, rather than formulating strategy top-down, based on a preset mission.
» ensuring the mission is linked to an analysis of the industry in which the company will have a major position. Management should investigate whether that particular industry will generate real returns to shareholders. Is this founded on industry attractiveness and can the company sustain a strong competitive position?

2. CREEPING BUSINESS COMPLEXITY

Managers are often busy destroying value through creeping business complexity. Whilst some may argue that Porter's competitive strategies are over-prescriptive and somewhat simplistic, he rightly stressed the need for:

» coherent strategic analysis; and
» the need to make explicit choices in how you are going to create superior value vis-à-vis the competition.

Increasing complexity may begin to destroy value, as this very complexity overreaches organizational capability and the learning capability of senior managers. Much of this value is destroyed by the costs of distraction of purpose – if you are pursuing a hundred and one product/market segments then you will be forever switching your attention and trying to adjust your operational recipes, whilst increasing costs and risks each time.

For example, one major drinks company acquired or developed new brands for its existing sales force. The theoretical extra volume failed to materialize basically because many of the sales force found it difficult to cope with the enlarged range.

The key lessons of how to avoid creeping business complexity are about the need:

» to put any new business opportunity through a "strategic screen" – probing it for the attractiveness of the market or niche, for its likely competitive position, its implementation capability, and also its financial scale and underlying attractiveness;
» to continually focus managers on making a few larger-scale projects work effectively, rather than seeking to diversify risk through lots of smaller projects;
» to continually revisit the business(es) we are in and in particular to set down the kinds of business we are *not* in (the most value added part of strategic choice is often to be able to say "no" to certain kinds of opportunity); and
» to map the complexity of the business by drawing up a matrix of products against markets against customer groups, or markets/customer

groups against distribution channels, and also against products with enabling technologies.

But the toughest job is that of the top team saying "no" to business opportunities which may seem tactically attractive but which may result in value destruction.

3. TACTICAL PRICING

We need look no further than the retail industry to recognize the perils of tactical pricing. In the UK retail supermarket industry, for example, there is a perpetual threat of price wars as the different players compete vigorously for market share in a maturing market.

There are several lessons on tactical pricing.

» When considering lower pricing this must be looked at as just *one* of the options to meet the strategic objective of protecting or growing profitable market share. Other options might include: market repositioning and enhancing customer service in ways which are known to add perceived and real value.
» Decisions to make major adjustments in price should take account of likely competitor reactions, then also of second-order company reactions, and in turn the second-order competitor reactions – that is, as a series of moves and not just as a single, one-off mechanical response.
» Where price reductions are contemplated, will they be big enough to secure the necessary shift in industry structure and behavior and to achieve competitive position?
» In some cases it may be appropriate to let go of market share which is less profitable or becoming increasingly difficult to defend. This runs against the heroic self-image of many management teams but it is just this ill-founded heroism which may destroy shareholder value in the long run.

4. BUSINESS INVESTMENT DECISIONS

Despite the wealth of prescriptive theory on capital and related investment decisions, management practices are often patchy and fragmented when it comes to integrating financial and strategic appraisal (see

Chapter 5). There are very many ways in which business investment decisions can destroy shareholder value; here are a few examples.

» Synergies are assumed but are not fully thought through in terms of when, under what conditions, and how they will be harvested.
» Less tangible factors, such as improving quality from the point of view of the customer, are assumed.
» Key uncertainties may exist which are not assessed. The appraisal may capture only the most obvious assumptions and miss those which are both of *high importance* and *high uncertainty*.
» The financial appraisal may suggest that apparently worthwhile projects do not yield a sufficient return to generate a positive net present value (NPV). Yet managers do not think, "Why is this?" It might be because the investment project simply maintains or protects the business's existing market position.

5. ACQUISITIONS

Acquisitions have been recognized as a graveyard area for corporate value, as we saw in Chapter 5. Corporate strategists have pointed out that many acquisitions are divested subsequently, often in a matter of a couple of years. In the 1990s there have been some spectacular corporate collapses of companies which have made inappropriate acquisitions and have either been taken over or gone into receivership. In other cases, like BT, acquisitions made in anticipation of market expansion were major destroyers of shareholder value – due to market and competitive setbacks.

Some key lessons for *not* destroying value via acquisitions are therefore:

» think through the acquisition strategy in depth and integrate the strategic, the operational, and the organizational and financial assumptions, testing these using the uncertainty–importance grid;
» use scenario tools and the importance–uncertainty grid to understand how value can be destroyed, to assess riskiness, and to reshape the strategy (both pre- and post-integration) to take into account the impact of variables which are both very important and very uncertain; and
» manage the deal-making and post-acquisition process with just as much care and attention as the pre-acquisition appraisal.

6. COST MANAGEMENT

Costs are frequently *not* regarded as a strategic issue, and often they are also managed in a very politicized and myopic way. Almost invariably, they are expressed (even in times of adversity and recession) as last year plus or minus a certain percentage.

Key routes to avoiding the destruction of value via cost management include the following.

» Targeting improvements in cost-effectiveness over a period of several years (not just via the annual budget cycle).
» Employing zero-based approaches to challenge the design of the business system – can the strategic objectives be achieved at much lower costs?
» Benchmarking existing competencies in allocating resources and in managing costs generally.
» Measuring the effect of value lost by poor quality or through error.
» Employing a "rob Peter to pay Paul" philosophy – to encourage re-allocation of resources. This reduces defensiveness to change, as people are less likely to defend what they are currently doing if there are some other activities which they can do and which add more value.
» Ensuring that changes in cost management are measured for *both* financial *and* competitive advantage. This sets a constraint on harmful cost cutting. In a high technology business a review of costs in its distribution function was achieved without detriment to customer service. This was achieved by cutting out unnecessarily frequent deliveries and charging a premium for value added, special deliveries.
» Be prepared to abandon a business strategy (or sub-strategy) where the company will not be able to compete due to inherent cost disadvantages.

7. CHANGE MANAGEMENT

One of the key costs of organizational life is unquestionably the cost of change. Change programs come in diverse forms – quality management, culture change, business process redesign, and many other interventions. These interventions are not always managed in a well-targeted way.

Although frameworks for managing change exist, many change programs:

» lack clear objectives and targeted benefits;
» are instigated as a result of only partial diagnosis of the problem; and
» are conceived of as "top-down" interventions which set up resistances, destroy value and increase costs.

Key ways of avoiding the destruction of shareholder value through change programs include the following.

» Managers proposing change projects or programs should be asked to produce a formal business case.
» The business case should lay out the strategic objectives of the change, and how it fits with and reinforces other change programs. These should also be supported by assumptions about implementation difficulty, likely resistances, and the adequacy of resources for the intervention. For example, at BP Amoco it was reported that a relatively small number of stories about breakthroughs in organizational behavior yielded shareholder value which was far greater than the cost of the culture change program.
» This business case should be used to promote and communicate the change, and to monitor the benefits and costs.

8. PRODUCT, BRAND, AND TECHNOLOGY DEVELOPMENT

Investment in product, brand, and technology development is crucial to long-term corporate health and shareholder value. Yet this investment is often either an act of faith or alternatively supported by spuriously accurate-looking cash flow projections. In the worst case, 80% of investment may be expended on the 20% of projects with *least* potential for competitive *and* financial benefit.

Key ways of avoiding this include the following.

» Assessing the company's capability to exploit a future opportunity through constructing a scenario of how that opportunity might crystallize. This should be followed by thinking through the *conditions* under which the scenario might crystallize. Management should then consider how realistic the company's assumptions are that it can exploit the opportunity operationally and for financial advantage.

» Evaluating the value of this capability as part of a set along with other capabilities – for instance, in marketing, production, and distribution. Capabilities require harvesting and without the right kind of support from the entire business system, value may not be yielded.

By asking the following questions.

» Where the development offers some major market breakthrough, will that market ultimately add shareholder value, and will this be sustained?
» Where will the company's sustainable share be?
» To what extent will customer value added be shared by the customer (due to high buyer power) versus the company?

9. OVER-COMMITMENT

Besides the eight "value destroyers" which we have now covered, there are two further ways in which shareholder value can be destroyed. These are more directly concerned with management processes. Firstly, the tendency towards early and over-commitment to particular projects or choices, and secondly, denial of error.

Over-commitment to a strategy can destroy value in a number of ways:

» too great an investment is committed to a particular strategy before management has achieved sufficient learning about the likely success of the strategy;
» when things begin to go wrong, there is denial that this is happening, or at least a "dampening down" of the bad news (see " Denial of corporate error" below);
» alternatively, more money, time, and effort is ploughed into the strategy to make it work (good money thus following bad), aggravating the misallocation of resources.

Key ways to manage commitment levels are:

» pilot new strategic moves – if possible try it out on a smaller basis first – to minimize shareholder value exposure;
» try to simulate what may happen, for example through classical scenario analysis – this should also include how shareholder value will be both created and captured;
» within the business case, expose the costs of any strategic retreat as part of the contingency plan, identifying ways of reducing exit costs;
» use away-days to give the senior team the time and thought-space to have a full and testing debate of key decisions; and
» deliberately build some flexibility into the strategic and financial decision. Flexibility in its own right actually does yield financial value, as taking on a series of projects over time reduces the risks of wasted resource.

10. DENIAL OF CORPORATE ERROR

Finally, there are the damaging effects of corporate error. These play a role across a wide range of decisions, acquisitions, internal developments, and change programs.

Over the past 10 years some of these corporate errors have been strategically and financially catastrophic – such as the expansion strategies of major telecoms businesses.

Factors which tend to promote denial of error include:

» *learning*: managers are often good at learning to improve performance in routine operational activities, but they are frequently quite poor at learning to do new things (especially complex ones) in new ways; and
» *leadership*: leaders may feel personally and unequivocally committed once they have set direction, notwithstanding change in the environment and also in what they are continually learning. Often this blockage is only removed by a change of leadership. This again introduces further lags and disruption into the management process, which in turn increase costs and destroy corporate value.

CONCLUSION

The issues of learning and leadership pose the biggest underlying threat to shareholder value, and thus supply us with clues as to how this can be avoided. These can only be tackled in an environment of no blame – not easy when companies are locked in a cycle of making and implementing decisions which often destroy shareholder value.

KEY LEARNING POINTS

» There are many different ways of avoiding shareholder value destruction – avoiding this requires the systematic and obsessive pursuit of shareholder value as a key corporate and business goal.
» This requires a considerable educative effort, a change of mind-set, and a culture change shift to achieve a number of key shifts as follows:
  » from short-term focus toward a more balanced trade-off between short- and long-term goals;
  » from the idea that growth is a good in itself to it being viewed as a contingent good – or merely as one of the set of value drivers; and
  » from a bias in favour of acquisitions towards more equal attention to different and complementary routes for corporate development.

Frequently Asked Questions (FAQs)

Q1: What is shareholder value and why is it different?

A: Chapter 1 and Chapter 2 explain in depth how shareholder value is used on short- and long-term cash flows, and is therefore different from accounting-based profit.

Q2: What are the different schools of thought regarding shareholder value?

A: Chapter 3 covers the evolution of shareholder value management.

Q3: What does "cost of capital" actually mean?

A: Chapter 2 and Chapter 3 show how to estimate the cost of capital.

Q4: What are the different approaches to calculating it?

A: Chapter 8 describes how different thinkers suggest the cost of capital should be calculated. Chapter 9 contains reference sources for getting the base data.

Q5: How is shareholder value created?

A: Chapter 3 and Chapter 6 look at the underlying drivers of shareholder value, which is illustrated with the case studies in Chapter 7 (especially that of Manchester United).

Q6: How should I set about evaluating investment projects?

A: Chapter 4 gives a comprehensive overview of the strategic investment decision problem.

Q7: What is the value generated from acquisitions?

A: Chapter 5 looks at acquisitions and shareholder value in an international context, particularly the BMW/Rover case.

Q8: How should the concept of shareholder value be implemented?

A: The success stories of BP Amoco and of IDV in Chapter 7 explain in depth the implications of implementing Value-Based Management approaches.

Q9: How should competitive change and uncertainties be dealt with in shareholder value calculations?

A: Chapter 6 takes you through the implications of change and uncertainty and how to deal with these.

Q10: What are the ways of destroying shareholder value, and how can these be resolved?

A: Chapter 10 takes us through the 10 ways in which shareholder value is most commonly destroyed, and how to avoid these.

Index

Printed and bound in the UK by
CPI Antony Rowe, Eastbourne

Printed and bound by CPI Group (UK) Ltd, Croydon, CR0 4YY

13/04/2025

14656564-0005